target archery

ADDISON-WESLEY PUBLISHING COMPANY
Reading, Massachusetts
Menlo Park, California · London · Amsterdam · Don Mills, Ontario · Sydney

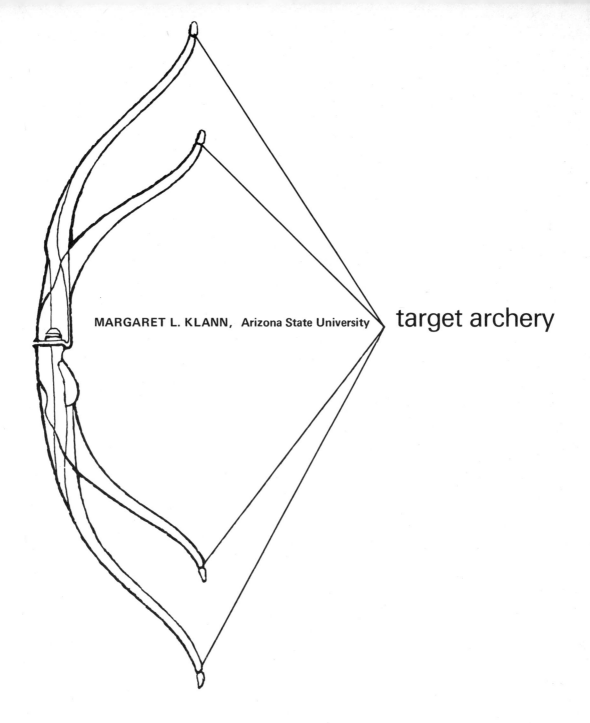

MARGARET L. KLANN, Arizona State University

target archery

This book is in the
ADDISON-WESLEY SERIES IN PHYSICAL EDUCATION
Katharine Ley
Consulting Editor

ISBN 0-201-03765-3
JKLMNOPQR-AL-798

preface

With the announcement in 1966 that for the first time in the history of the modern Olympic Games target archery would be included as a gold medal sport in the 1972 summer games, there has been a sudden, strong revival of interest in club, camp, high school, and collegiate target archery.

The National Archery Association has encouraged this movement by establishing a Junior Olympic Development Program under the direction of Mr. George Helwig of Cincinnati, Ohio. This program is designed to encourage participation in target archery and to hold the interest of boys and girls ages 8 to 18. It has grown each year and has been a most important factor in the emergence of young boys and girls as United States team members for competitive purposes.

Believing that the United States Olympic Team should be trained at the collegiate level in archery, as it is in so many other sports, Miss Lorraine Pszczola of San Bernardino, California, has devised a "College Development Program." This is similar to the Junior Olympic program, but is based on the FITA Round and scoring system. Through participation in this program, collegiate target archers will be encouraged to begin and continue with the sport, and at the same time become familiar with the rules and scoring that will be used in Olympic competition.

The number of collegiate mail, telegraphic and shoulder-to-shoulder archery meets has steadily increased in the past five years. The staging of the First United States Intercollegiate Championships at Tempe, Arizona, in 1967, came as an indication of the renewed interest in collegiate target archery. In this historic meet, there were 63 men and women shooting, representing 19 colleges and 7 states. The final scores of the champions, John Culver of Fresno (California) State College and Lois Ruby Burcaw of Michigan State University, indicated that the target archers to be found in colleges and universities in the United States now will be strong contenders for places on future United States teams. As instruction improves and competitive opportunities become more numerous, scores will climb and the competition for places on the U.S. teams will become even keener.

However, one of the main problems which must be solved as quickly as possible, if the quality of target archery instructional programs is to be continuously upgraded, is that of helping archery students, teachers, and coaches to become better prepared to do their jobs, and to understand the problems concerned with learning and teaching target archery. The National Archery Association, the Professional Archers Association, and several universities have joined the Teela-Wooket Archery Camp in providing centers for courses designed to improve instruction in archery, and as the number of training centers increases, the quality of archery instruction will improve.

This book is written to meet the need for an up-to-date reference for target archers of any age, in school or out. No attempt has been made to evolve a new technique of shooting, or a new sure method of teaching yourself or others how to shoot. The materials included were collected over a period of almost a quarter of a century of teaching and coaching high school and collegiate target archers and working with teachers and coaches. The book includes a presentation of long-established principles of target archery which have proved to be basic to good shooting with a bow and arrow. Most of today's outstanding target archers are using the techniques presented here, and the information should be of use to beginning as well as skilled archers who do not have the services of a coach. The book would also be most appropriate for target archery classes in high schools, camps, or colleges.

ACKNOWLEDGMENTS

So many people have helped me in the preparation of this book (sometimes without knowing they were doing so), that it would be an impossible task to list and individually thank the hundreds whose influence is reflected in the pages which follow.

How could I possibly thank each of the students in archery classes in the past 25 years, who have asked questions seeking added information or clarification, and who, by so doing, kindled the spark for the idea of this book?

How could I repay with words the confidence expressed by those students who, after a semester of archery instruction, stopped by the desk when the last class was over and asked "Why don't you write a book on archery?"

There is no possible way I could list the many people at tournaments who have spent hours helping me to understand some of the minute and exacting details of this fascinating sport.

Could I list the many friends who have been a constant source of inspiration as they prodded me into trying new things, and who have patiently listened to me or who have given up free time to accompany me on necessary archery trips?

The National Archery Association of the United States, through its Executive Secretary, Clayton Shenk, has been most generous in allowing the reproduction of the official rules; and the Archery Manufacturers Organization enthusiastically granted permission, through its Executive Secretary, John Lanigan, to include the new terminology and standards for the manufacture of archery equipment.

A word of grateful appreciation must go to my colleague, Dr. William Stone, Assistant Professor of Physical Education, Arizona State University, for writing the chapter on the scientific aspects of archery; and to Judy Severance, a former archery "great" at Arizona State University, go special thanks for her chapter on the history of archery and much of the glossary. I am indebted to both of them for their continued interest and their encouragement when the going got rough.

Charles Conley has done a magnificent job of the illustrative photographs. He has a "feel" for archery and beautifully captures its essence on film. Kirstie Kaiser, a Physical Education major at Arizona State University, is the model who made Mr. Conley's work come to life. Her skill, as well as her pride in being an integral part of archery, is evident. She is one of the top collegiate archers in the United States, and I am grateful to her for allowing us to photographically capture her fine archery technique.

A word of deep appreciation must go to Max Hamilton for permission to use ideas he expressed in past issues of *The Archer's Magazine* and *Archery World*. To both him and his wife Jewel go thanks for their continued friendship and enthusiastic support.

To Al Henderson, a friend of many years and the man who always has time to help me solve my archery problems, goes my deep gratitude. His suggestions concerning the chapter on equipment were most helpful and his words of praise have kept the feeble fire alive many times.

The articles written by Bill Webb, which appeared in *Archery World,* were drawn upon for the chapter on how an arrow flies. His style of writing makes it all seem so simple, and I am grateful to him for presenting his ideas so clearly.

Any author writing a book of this kind would be remiss if he did not gratefully acknowledge the twenty or more years of dedicated and inspirational work done by Myrtle and Ed Miller, Directors of the Teela-Wooket Archery Camp, Roxbury, Vermont. They have held fast to their belief that archers and archery teachers needed and wanted help, in order to better prepare themselves and to more thoroughly understand the intricacies of this sport. Their June camp has been rightly called "The Archery Training Center of The World," and having been a one-time student there, I am grateful to both of them for their continued interest and encouragement.

Many of the ideas expressed in the chapter on tackle setup were adapted from the 1968 Easton Aluminum Arrow brochure, and I am grateful to Doug Easton for permission to use this material.

To Gretchen James, another of my former archery "greats" and one who has never lost interest or faith, my sincere thanks for all the kind words and thoughts, and my appreciation for reading chapter after chapter and making suggestions concerning them.

My friends, colleagues, and students have made heroic efforts to help me understand archery, and to clarify what I have written. They have patiently listened, and then made suggestions and corrections. Any mistakes which appear on these pages must therefore be attributed to my own inability to convey the correct information in words.

Tempe, Arizona   M.L.K.
December 1969

contents

Lois Ruby, Michigan State University, takes a look back at intercollegiate archery.

looking back at archery

Evidence of the use of the bow and arrow can be traced back to the prehistoric man of at least 25,000 years ago, and it is quite prominent throughout the entire history of man, so trying to relate the history of archery in one chapter is like trying to condense the history of man into one chapter.

The records concerning the origin of the bow are incomplete and vague and probably we will never have completely accurate details. One of the most widely accepted theories states that after man learned to throw a shaft, he devised the bow as a way of propelling it farther and with more force. Another theory states that it was derived from a "sling shot" method of hurling rocks using vines and young trees.

The bow and fire are considered to be the two greatest influences in the rise of man above the beasts, and until the introduction of gunpowder, the bow was the most important weapon in warfare.

Evidence of the use of the bow has been found in every country of the world. Even the Australians used a very short bow and tiny arrows dipped in poison. Cave drawings show hunters using bows, and animals with arrows piercing their bodies. A study of these drawings indicates that the bow was a vital part of their religion, elaborate ceremonial rites having been performed before a hunt to ensure success.

Many past civilizations refer to the bow in writings concerning their religious rituals, and even in our modern times some tribes among the Mexican and American Indians conduct some ceremonies involving the bow and arrow. According to the Bible, the Israelites and Assyrians were great archers and the Babylonians, Greeks, Persians, and Egyptians also favored the sport.

Probably the best-known references to archery occur in ancient Roman and Greek mythology. Apollo, God of Archery, once mocked Cupid, God of Love, saying that he was a boy playing with a man's weapon. The enraged Cupid decided to get his revenge by shooting Apollo with the golden arrow of love, causing him to fall in love with Daphne. Cupid then shot Daphne with the lead arrow of hate, causing her to hate Apollo so much that she turned herself into a laurel tree upon which Apollo later hung his bow as a tribute to his lost love.

In other literature we find many classic references extolling the skill of archers. William Tell was a Swiss archer who shot an apple from the top of his son's head using a crossbow; Longfellow's poem, "The Song of Hiawatha," combines archery fact and fiction; Cooper wrote stories of the American Indians and their prowess with the bow and arrow; and probably the most noted piece of archery literature is the story of the legendary Robin Hood, whose feats were amazing, but questionable. Other works in which reference is made to archery include *The Iliad* and *The Odyssey, Macbeth,* and *Gulliver's Travels.*

There are numerous works of art centered around archery, including sculptured figures, paintings, and drawings, as well as the famous Bayeux Tapestry. On this band of linen

23 inches wide and 231 feet long, the women whose men were away fighting the Battle of Hastings embroidered the complete story of the battle as they received news of it day by day.

The history of archery in England is most interesting and had great influence on the development of the sport in the United States. The English "longbow" is the most famous of all bows. The forerunner of this bow came from Wales rather than England; the Welsh bow was shorter and heavier and at times it was used as a club. The English adopted the bow and modified it, creating the six-foot "longbow" made of yew wood. Yew wood was in such great demand by bowyers and archers that King Edward I issued a decree prohibiting the sale of yew outside England. Merchant ships returning to England were even required to bring a load of yew staves so that there would be enough seasoned wood to keep the English army supplied with bows for warfare.

In 1545 Roger Ascham wrote the first book on archery, *Toxophilus.* King Henry VIII was so impressed with the work that he gave Ascham a pension of ten pounds per year and appointed him as instructor to the court. He then issued a decree that required every male from the ages of 7 to 60 to own and practice with a bow. He also required that targets be placed throughout the towns so that the men would have something to shoot at that would not shoot back. The required shooting distance was 200 yards, and any man caught shooting less was fined.

Through a brief review of some of the famous battles in English history, we can trace the chronological advancement of the bow as a weapon of war. Between 850 and 950 A.D., the Vikings invaded England and attacked from the coast with great volleys of arrows before going ashore. Later, in 1066, the Normans faked a retreat during the Battle of Hastings, drawing the English out into the open where they suffered a costly defeat. In 1252 England adopted the longbow as its national weapon and, remembering the Normans' tactics, defeated the French in the Hundred Years War. The bow and arrow remained the chief weapon of war until 1588, when firearms and gunpowder replaced the bow during the invasion of the Spanish Armada.

The English interest and influence in archery was transferred to the United States when five men organized the first archery club, The United Bowmen of Philadelphia, on September 3, 1828. One week later they held their first target practice, and in 1829 they conducted their first championship tournament. Shooting was done from a distance of 80 yards, but historical records make no mention of the number of arrows shot or the winning score. In 1833 the tournament was shot by time rather than by the number of ends, and in the 1835 meet, the York Round was adopted and became standard for competitive purposes.

Tournaments then differed from those of today in that they were more formal and the shooting was only a part of the day's activity. Detailed minutes were recorded at each meeting and even the conversation at dinner was noted. In those days each archer was identified by a symbol rather than by name, and this symbol was used on scoreboards as well as in the minutes. The symbol chosen by each archer was related to his vocation: the doctor used a crossbones, the sea captain an anchor, the bowyer an arrow, etc. Tournament procedure called for the use of the English plan. A target was placed at each end of the range. The archers started at one end and shot three arrows down range; they then scored them and shot them back to the other end. This style was originally adopted because of a lack of good quality arrows, each archer probably having no more than three good arrows at any one time.

The United Bowmen of Philadelphia remained active for a period of 30 years. The following 20 years showed a marked decline of interest in archery, but by 1878 numerous new clubs were being formed and it was decided that a governing body should be organized. The National Archery Association of the United States was formed on January 23, 1879, and held its first tournament in August of that year. The meet was held in the baseball park of the Chicago White Stockings, where because of the location of the seating area for spectators, targets could be placed at only one end of the field. Because of English tradition the archers wished to shoot only three arrows at a time, so they devised and put into use the "three and three" system used in most major archery tournaments today. In this arrangement each archer has six arrows; he shoots three of them and then relinquishes his place on the shooting line to a target mate, who also shoots three arrows. The first archer then shoots his remaining three arrows, and is followed again by his target mate. It is interesting to note that the English did not adopt this system until the middle of the twentieth century!

Although target archery is continually growing in popularity as a sport, the bow and arrow is being used in other ways. The British army still employs a unit of archers as the Queen's bodyguard, and the bow is being used extensively by the U.S. forces in Vietnam and other war areas. Many primitive tribes still use the bow as their weapon of survival, and it is quite popular as a hunting weapon in the United States, where many states provide a special season exclusively for archers.

Interest in the sport will continue to increase as indoor ranges become available in all parts of the country. Many new tournaments are now being conducted, not only on the state and national levels but on the international level as well. In September of 1968, the first European championships were held in Austria and, as far as is known, this meet marked the first international competitive appearance of any woman from Russia. In 1972 target archery will again become a part of the Olympic Games, not merely as a demonstration sport as it was in the early 1900's but as a gold medal event. This fact has triggered a renewal of interest in and dedication to target archery all over the world.

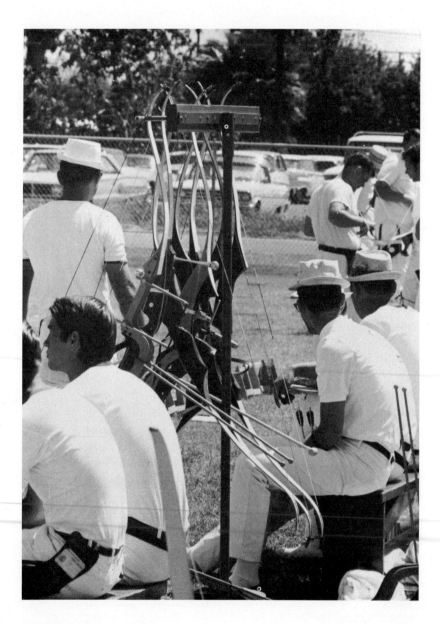

All kinds of archery equipment.

target archery equipment

If you were a nonarcher glancing at a current archery equipment catalogue or viewing a display at a tackle shop, you might be overwhelmed by the vast number of items you would see. Your first reaction would probably be: "If target archery takes all of that equipment, I can't afford it."[1] You would have a right to be dismayed, for in no other sport are there so many pieces of equipment needed, nor so many extra "gadgets" available. However, if you made inquiries you would find that to learn to shoot a bow and arrow very little equipment is needed; a bow with a sight attached to it, six or eight arrows, an armguard, a finger tab, and a target with a face on it are sufficient. You could postpone buying even this much if an indoor archery lane establishment was available where you could rent equipment until you decided what kind and how much you wanted. When you finally decide to get your own tackle, purchase the best you can afford, because it

---

1.   Retail prices of equipment are listed at the end of the chapter.

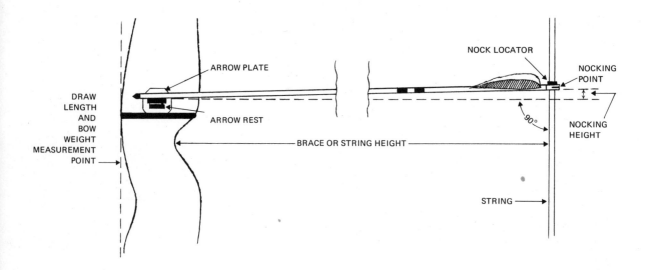

DRAW LENGTH AND BOW WEIGHT MEASUREMENT POINT →

ARROW PLATE

ARROW REST

NOCK LOCATOR

NOCKING POINT

NOCKING HEIGHT

BRACE OR STRING HEIGHT

90°

STRING →

Fig. 2-1 Bow terminology.

pays off in accuracy and will last longer. Surprising as it may seem, the quality of the arrows is more important than the quality of the bow. It is possible for a good archer to shoot high scores with an average bow and excellent arrows, but no matter how highly skilled he is or how good his bow is his scores will immediately drop when he changes to poor arrows.

In a book such as this it would be an impossible task to discuss all the kinds of equipment available, so we will confine ourselves to the most important items.[2]

ARCHERY TERMINOLOGY

In the past as you read archery books and catalogues you may have noted that there was considerable difference in the terminology used. It seems that some terms meant different things to different people, and this had led to much confusion.

---

2. Throughout this book, it is assumed that the reader is right-handed.

This confusion developed over a period of several centuries. Terms which were meaningful in the 1500's no longer have any real meaning. "Fistmele" is a good example. At one time, bows had a brace-height which was roughly the width of the hand with the thumb extended upward. This was called "fistmele." Today there are practically no bows which use this low a brace-height and so this term has no real meaning and is very confusing to everyone.

In 1968 the Archery Manufacturers Organization (AMO) and others announced the adoption of a set of standards for equipment and a set of standardized terms, with the hope that as they became known they would be adopted by all who are concerned with archery in its many forms. The terminology used in this book is that adopted by the AMO. The names for the parts of the bow, arrow, and string are shown in Figs. 2-1 through 2-5. Standards for equipment will be mentioned under each individual piece, as they are discussed on pages which follow.

BOWS

Target archery bows have assumed several different shapes (Fig. 2-6). The old and historic longbow, made famous by the English soldiers of the fifteenth century, is seldom used today, and static recurve and reflex bows are becoming harder to find. However, each served its purpose in the steps which led to the development of today's most accurate bow, the working recurve.

In this book we will confine ourselves to a discussion of the working recurve and its less expensive variation, the semirecurve, since in most instances these are the bows which will be purchased or used.

Bows used to be made from wood because that was the best material available. These bows were smooth-shooting and

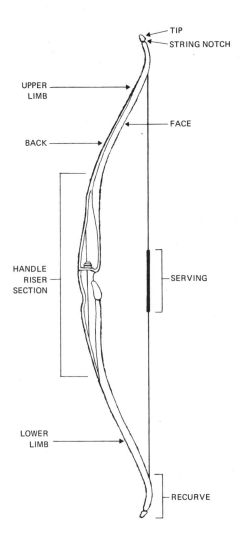

Fig. 2-2 Parts of the bow.

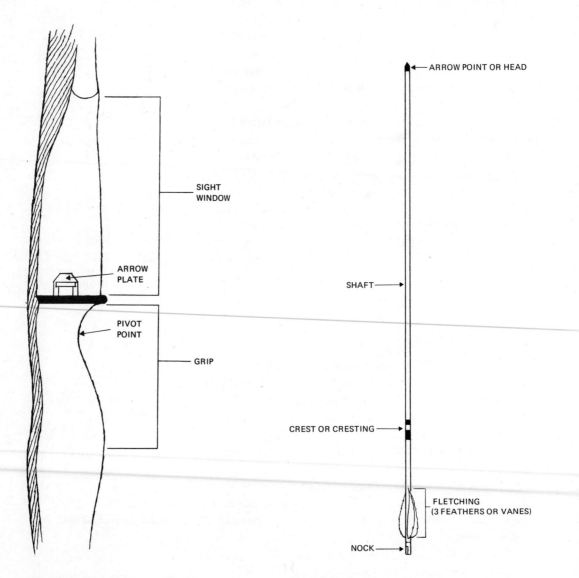

SIGHT
WINDOW

ARROW
PLATE

PIVOT
POINT

GRIP

ARROW POINT OR HEAD

SHAFT

CREST OR CRESTING

FLETCHING
(3 FEATHERS OR VANES)

NOCK

Fig. 2-3 Parts of the bow, continued.

Fig. 2-4 Parts of the arrow.

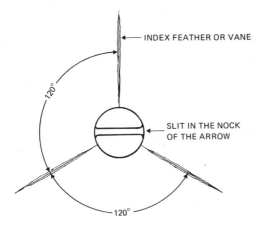

Fig. 2-5 Placement of the feathers on the shaft.

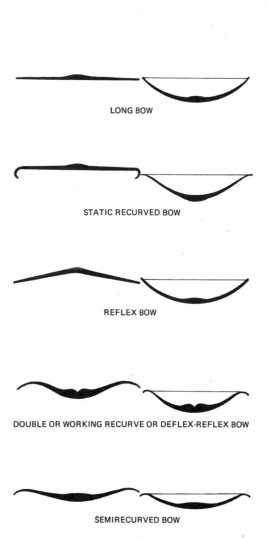

LONG BOW

STATIC RECURVED BOW

REFLEX BOW

DOUBLE OR WORKING RECURVE OR DEFLEX-REFLEX BOW

SEMIRECURVED BOW

Fig. 2-6 Shapes of bows.

accurate at short distances, but they lacked cast[3] and were affected by changes in weather. They were brittle on cold days, lost cast on hot days, and warped on wet days. With the invention of fiberglass came the molded bow made entirely of that substance. These were less expensive than wooden bows, they had good cast, and weather did not affect them, but they vibrated and "kicked" upon release and this caused many inaccurate shots. Bowyers then decided to try making a bow using both wood and fiberglass to see if the advantages of each could be captured and their disadvantages overcome. Wood was used for the main body of the bow with a thin layer of fiberglass on both the face and back. This is the bow which is called a *composite* bow today; it is smooth-shooting, has good cast, and is almost immune to weather conditions. Practically all composite bows made today are working recurves or some variation of that shape. These are bows which have been used to shoot the fantastically high scores of the past few years.

---

3. The speed which a bow can impart to an arrow.

Bow manufacturers are constantly at work trying new ideas to produce better-shooting bows. Fairly recently a metal handle-riser section was introduced, and the weight thus added to the bow gave greater stability to the bow arm and resulted in higher scores. A short time ago a bow with pulleys was introduced and although many people disliked its looks, it had the distinct advantage of becoming easier to pull as you drew near your anchor spot. Several kinds of true center shot bows have been marketed recently, and numerous tournaments have been won by archers using them. With this kind of bow the upper limb is designed so that the arrow rests exactly in the middle of the bow rather than somewhat to the left of the center.

It is entirely possible that new bow designs will make the composite working recurve obsolete in a few years, but at the moment it is the finest bow made.

Bowyers have also produced the less expensive composite semirecurved bow. This is not quite as smooth-shooting and lacks the fine cast of the working recurve, but it is ideal for school and camp use and has proved highly satisfactory to many tournament archers as well.

When we speak of the *weight* of the bow, we mean the number of pounds of energy it takes to draw the string back a specified distance. Unless a bow is marked otherwise, weights are measured at 28 inches. Thus, if a bow is marked "26 lb," it means that it takes 26 pounds of energy to draw the string back 28 inches, but if the marking is "30 lb @ 26"," the bow weight has been measured with the string drawn only 26 inches.

Bows vary in weight from 10 to 125 pounds. The 10- and 15-pounders would be ideal for eight- and nine-year-olds, or even for an adult who lacks the strength to draw more weight than that with ease and comfort. The 125-pound bow would probably be used by an elephant hunter who would only have to draw it once during a day, if he was lucky enough to get sufficiently close for a shot at an elephant. There is no rule in target archery which places a limit on the bow weight to be used; however, in actual practice, they are seldom heavier than 45 pounds. This is simply because a target archer in a practice session or tournament may shoot 70 or more arrows, with little rest between shots. He is therefore using the same finger, arm, shoulder, and back muscles over and over again, with resulting fatigue. When he is tired, he is shaky and he lacks the ability to make his body parts do what he wants them to. Both these factors affect the accuracy of his shooting and his scores begin to drop. In order to obtain high scores, it is therefore better to use a bow which the archer can accurately handle for several hours of shooting rather than a bow which will give him high scores only for those few ends before he becomes tired.

The most common mistake made in the selection of a bow is to choose one that is too heavy in the draw weight *for the person who is going to be using it.* Many misguided department store clerks, school purchasing agents, camp directors, physical education teachers, and coaches choose bows which to them seem easy to pull but which will be too difficult for their students to draw comfortably. It is far better to begin with a light bow which is realistically within your strength and endurance to draw and hold without undue strain. You can then *easily* draw the string back and your mind and body are left free to develop *good* shooting habits from the very beginning. This is another reason why it is advisable to begin by renting tackle; you can start with a lightweight bow and as your strength increases, you can use a bow of a heavier weight until you find the weight you want to use.

Schools and camps should supply beginning archers with lightweight bows for class use and as an archer achieves greater skill, he should be encouraged to purchase his own equipment (Fig. 2-7).

Even though bows are usually measured for weight at 28 inches, not all archers draw that length arrow. In these cases, the *actual weight* of the bow with their length draw is

Age, years	Boys and Men	Girls and Women
8 to 10	10-15 lb	10-15 lb
11 to 15	15-20 lb	15-20 lb
16 to 19	25-30 lb	20-25 lb
20 and up	30 lb and up	25 lb and up

Fig. 2-7 Recommended draw weights for target archery bows.

different from that marked on the bow. If an archer wishes to buy arrows that are matched to the weight of his bow (see Chapter 7), he must determine what his actual draw-weight is. The AMO standard system for figuring this is:

1. Divide the marked weight on the bow by 20, carrying the division out to two decimal places.

   Example: your bow is marked; "35 lb @ 28"," but you are only drawing 25 inches.

   $$\frac{35 \text{ lb}}{20} = 1.75 \text{ lb}.$$

2. Determine how many inches less than 28 inches you are drawing, and multiply the answer from Step 1 above by that number.

28 in.	1.75 lb
25 in.	× 3
3 in. less	5.25 lb

3. Subtract the answer from Step 2 above from the marked weight of the bow. This gives you your *actual draw-weight* with your 25-inch arrow.

   35.00 lb weight marked on the bow
   − 5.25 lb

   29.75 lb your actual draw weight

   Note: in this system, if you were using an arrow that was longer than 28 inches, you would *add* the answer you got in Step 2 to the weight marked on the bow.

   Example: you are drawing 30 inches on a bow marked 35 lb @ 28".

   Step 2. you are drawing 2 inches more:
   1.75 lb × 2 = 3.50 lb
   Step 3. 35 lb plus 3.50 lb = 38.5 lb
   your actual draw-weight with
   a 30-in. arrow.

Target archery bows vary from 52 to 72 inches in length, and have been available in 2-inch increments. As a part of their standardization plan the AMO has agreed to make all their bows in one-inch increments beginning in 1968.

The bow length needed by an individual is determined largely but not exclusively by the length arrow to be used with the bow. Young boys and girls, and short adults would normally use the shorter bows, because the height of a person has a great deal to do with the length of arrows he needs. Tall people usually have longer arms than short people and would require longer arrows. If a person who required 30-inch arrows were to use a 52-inch bow, he would find his three string fingers being pinched at full-draw, due to the acute angle formed by the string (Fig. 2-8).

There used to be a belief that the longer bows did not have as good a cast as the shorter ones, but this is not necessarily true with the bows manufactured today. Most men prefer bows 66 to 70 inches long, and most women choose bows 62 to 66 inches long. The shorter ones are used by younger boys and girls, and in schools and camps.

Bowstrings

Today most bowstrings are made of dacron because this has proved to be a long lasting material which stretches comparatively little.

Strings which have one loop in them are called "single-looped" strings and they are used on longbows (Fig. 2-6). The loop is placed near the upper notch, and the string is then tied into the lower notch with a timber hitch. Adjustments are made until the proper brace height is reached.

A string which is to be used on any kind of recurved bow must be a "double-looped" string; it must have a loop at each end. If you were to use a single-looped string on such a bow, the knot holding the string in the lower notch would rub

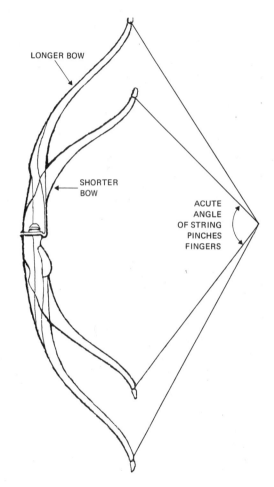

LONGER BOW

SHORTER BOW

ACUTE ANGLE OF STRING PINCHES FINGERS

Figure 2-8

against the recurved tip each time the string was released. This would result in friction, which in turn would cause the string to break.

A double-looped string must be exactly the correct length for the bow on which it will be used, to get the brace-height (Fig. 2-3) recommended by the manufacturer. Each bowyer has determined, through experimentation, the brace-height giving the greatest efficiency with the various models of his bow. Go along with his recommendation until you prove to yourself that another brace-height is better for *you*. It is important that the brace-height always be the same; measure it and make a note of it, and then measure it each time you brace your bow, making adjustments if they are needed. Double-looped strings can be shortened slightly by twisting them a little more, but never put more than 12 full twists in a string or it will kink and break quickly. To slightly lengthen a double-looped string, untwist it a few turns.

The biggest problem with bowstrings in the past has been getting the correct length. If you went into a store and asked for a double-looped string to fit a 62-inch, 30-pound bow, chances are that the one you bought wouldn't give you the brace-height you wanted. No two bowstring makers made them the same length for 62-inch bows and there might be as much as two inches difference between the lengths of two strings. The only way you could be sure that the string fit properly would be to take the bow to the shop and try it on the bow.

The AMO, beginning in 1968, has agreed to make all their bowstrings in one-inch increments, and to mark each string with the draw-weight it is designed for and the length bow it will fit. All AMO standard made strings marked 62 inches will fit all AMO standard made bows marked 62 inches. It will be the bow manufacturers' responsibility to see that the bow length and the corresponding string length give the proper brace-height. A word of caution, however; archers must remember that not *all* archery equipment is made by firms belonging to AMO, but whatever is will be marked "AMO Standard."

Lightweight bows take a comparatively thin bowstring, but if the same string were used on a heavyweight hunting bow, it would quickly break. How many strands of dacron do you need for a particular bow? The manufacturer of dacron makes the following recommendations:

Using either "Regular B" or "Super B", bonded (unwaxed) or waxed string:

For bows 20-30 lb, use 8 strands.
For bows 25-35 lb, use 10 strands.
For bows 35-45 lb, use 12 strands.
For bows 45-55 lb, use 14 strands.
For bows 55-80 lb, use 16 strands.

Some expert archers prefer a string with two strands less than the recommendation. This gives them a "faster" string, and makes it possible to get four or five more yards distance with their bow. Of course, these strings break more quickly because they are so thin.

A bowstring should have no more serving on it than is necessary to protect the dacron from friction at the loop ends (about 3½ inches) and from the fingers, arrow, and armguard at the nocking point (about 5 inches total; 1½ inches above the nock-locator and 3½ inches below it). Any additional serving is excess weight and makes for a sluggish string, which cuts down on the distance your bow will propel the arrow.

Nylon is commonly used for servings, but some archers prefer monofilament fishing line since it gives the arrows a smoother get-away and doesn't get fuzzy and worn from rubbing against the armguard.

Stabilizers

A stabilizer often looks like a metal rod screwed into the back of the bow and extending outward from it. On the end of the rod is a knob about one inch in diameter. The addition of one or more stabilizers to a bow is probably the main reason for the extremely high scores being shot by tournament archers today. Earl Hoyt, Jr., conceived this idea a number of years ago. He began by adding a lead weight internally to the grip section of the bow. This weight added stability to the bow because it reduced bow arm movement. Scores immediately began to climb, and so a whole series of additional experiments with stabilizers was conducted. From these came the idea of extending the weight out from the bow. With the weight on a rod three to five inches outward from the bow, the bow would turn more slowly in the archer's hand if he was torquing the bow the least bit. This would allow the arrow to clear the bow before it *began* to turn so that its flight would not be affected by the torquing. Stabilizers as long as 28 inches have been used successfully, and whether there should be one or two stabilizers and what their length should be are points that archers argue at great length. Some stabilizers can be adjusted to the length you desire; others are not adjustable at all. Some have a soft coupler where the rod joins the bow, others have a stiff one, and some couplers are adjustable. Which stabilizer is best for you? This is a matter of personal preference, and is based on the combination of your bow, arrows, string, nock-locator, arrow rest, and personal shooting style. You must try various ones to determine which one gives you the best groups on the target face, and it is possible that you will have to make minor adjustments in the distance the weight is from your bow in order to achieve the greatest benefits.

It must be remembered that not all working recurved bows come equipped with stabilizers, this advantage is found only on the more expensive models.

Bowsights

A bowsight is a device attached to your bow which aims the point of your arrow both horizontally and vertically. Whether

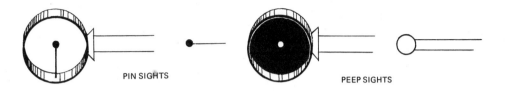

PIN SIGHTS

PEEP SIGHTS

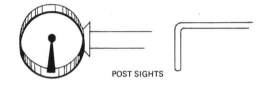

POST SIGHTS

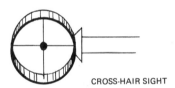

CROSS-HAIR SIGHT

Fig. 2-9 Types of bowsights.

you mount your sight on the back or face of your bow is a matter of personal preference. Those who like it on the back say they get a clearer view of the sight because it is two or three inches farther from their eyes. Those who prefer it on the face believe that it is easier to adjust since you do not have to turn your bow around to get to it, and that you get additional yardage because the bowsight is closer to your eye.

There are four basic types of bowsights: pin sights, post sights, peep sights, and cross-hair sights (Fig. 2-9). These are all single sights. There are also double sights; that is, you have two bowsights, one in front of the other with the distances between them varying from six inches to two feet. Double sights operate on the same principle as a rifle with a front and rear sight, and make aiming more accurate.

ARROWS

The shafts of arrows are made of wood, fiberglass, or aluminum. The wood most preferred is Port Orford cedar, and practically all wooden shafts being made today are of this wood. Highly skilled archers do not use wooden shafts because it is so difficult to find a dozen or more that will match each other in weight and spine[4] due to differences in grain and density. It is entirely possible that wooden arrows will be obsolete in a few years.

Since fiberglass is a machine-manufactured product, the shafts can be more closely matched in spine and weight, and they will shoot much more accurately than wooden arrows. Fiberglass shafts will stand a lot of abuse; weather has no effect upon them, it is hard to break them, and it is even hard to put a bend in them. However, if they come from the manufacturer with a bent shaft, it is very difficult to straighten them because to do so you must heat the fiberglass, and the melting point is so critical that if you apply the least bit too much heat you will melt the shaft. Educational groups would do well to investigate the possibilities of buying fiberglass arrows for class use, for even though they are initially more expensive than wood they last longer and give greater accuracy.

The highly skilled archer should use aluminum shafts since they are by far the most accurate. They are comparatively light and can be matched perfectly in spine and weight. They are the most expensive kind of shaft, and they can become bent during use if they hit wood, rocks, or hard objects. There are, however, numerous arrow straighteners on the market and most of them do a good job of taking the bends out of a shaft.

The length of an arrow is measured from the bottom of the slit in the nock to the back of the point (Fig. 2-10). This is another part of the AMO standardization plan.

The arrow length needed by an archer is determined by the length of his arms. There are several methods of measuring

---

4. The amount an arrow will bend.

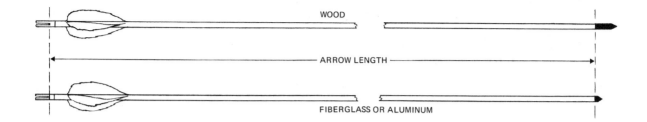

WOOD

ARROW LENGTH

FIBERGLASS OR ALUMINUM

for the length needed, but probably one of the simplest is as follows:

Fig. 2-10 The measurement of arrows.

1. Have a partner place the end of a yardstick against your breastbone.
2. Extend both of your arms sideward at shoulder height. Now bring them forward parallel to the ground, without stretching or reaching, until they touch the yardstick.
3. Have your partner note where your fingertips touch the yardstick. This is the correct length arrow for you.

Another, more accurate method, is to have the archer draw and properly anchor with an arrow which has been marked off in 1-inch increments starting at the slit in the nock and working toward the point. He should make sure that his left arm is in a good shooting position. A partner can then note which inch-mark is lined up with the back of the bow.

It is important to start beginners with arrows which are long enough for them, because if an arrow is overdrawn and released, serious injury can result. It is safer to give a beginner arrows which are two inches too long for him than arrows which are a little too short for him. After a few lessons he can be fitted with arrows of the proper length. Efficiency is lost if he continues to shoot with arrows which are too long for him.

LEATHER OR PLASTIC;
ONE HOOK; ELASTIC BANDS.

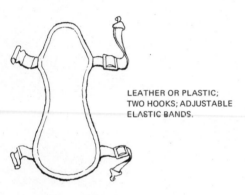

LEATHER OR PLASTIC;
TWO HOOKS; ADJUSTABLE
ELASTIC BANDS.

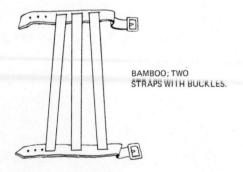

BAMBOO; TWO
STRAPS WITH BUCKLES.

Fig. 2-11 Armguards.

For accurate shooting your arrows must be matched to the draw-weight of your bow. This allows you to shoot an arrow which has just the right amount of spine so that it clears the bow and flies perfectly. More information on this topic will be found in Chapter 7.

ACCESSORIES

Armguards

Armguards come in a variety of shapes and sizes, and may be made from leather, plastic, bamboo, etc. (Fig. 2-11). All armguards serve two main purposes, the most important of which is to protect your bow forearm from being hit by the string. They also hold long sleeves close to your arm so that the string will not be interfered with on its forward movement.

An armguard should be thick enough to give the desired protection and pliable enough that it can be made to fit the shape of your arm. It should also be adjustable to allow for the differences in the thickness of arms.

Finger Protection

The two most widely used types of protection for your string fingers are finger tabs and shooting gloves. Both are designed to protect your fingers from abrasion and to provide a smoother release (Fig. 2-12).

Tabs are the more popular kind with target archers because they are more pliable, can be easily cut down in size to fit your fingers and give a smoother release. In general, they are made of cordovan leather or unborn calf skin and may be one, two, or three layers thick. Some kinds even include a layer of felt. Probably the most common mistake is to use a

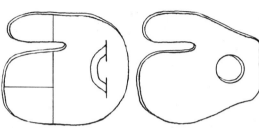  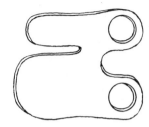

TAB WITH LEATHER
THONG LOOP TO GO OVER
YOUR MIDDLE FINGER

TAB WITH SINGLE HOLE
THROUGH WHICH YOU
PUT YOUR MIDDLE FINGER

TAB WITH TWO HOLES, ONE FOR
THE INDEX FINGER AND THE OTHER
FOR THE MIDDLE AND RING FINGERS

TAB WITH TWO HOLES, ONE
FOR THE INDEX FINGER AND THE
OTHER FOR THE RING FINGER

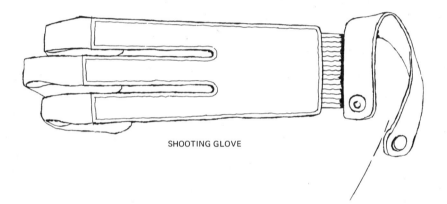

Fig. 2-12 Finger protection.

SHOOTING GLOVE

finger tab that is too big. The more excess leather there is on your tab, the more difficult it becomes for the string to slide smoothly over and clear the tab as you release. Most tabs are too long and should be trimmed down until there is just enough protection for your finger tips as you release. Some tabs are too wide and should be trimmed down so that they do not extend outside the edges of your three string fingers.

Shooting gloves are preferred by some archers because they surround the entire finger and give more protection, especially between the index and middle fingers, where soreness often develops due to the hard contact with the nock. Cordovan or elkskin is most commonly used for shooting gloves because it is firm enough to give a smooth release and thick enough to give the desired protection.

Quivers

Target archers seem to prefer some kind of hip quiver to hold their arrows when they are shooting, but some will choose either a pocket or shoulder quiver (Fig. 2-13).

Ground quivers which hold both bow and arrows are often used in school and camp instructional classes. Many tournament target archers also use one to keep their bow off the ground while they are at the target scoring.

TARGET EQUIPMENT

Target Matts and Butts

Target matts are made of two materials; marsh grass and excelsior. They are alike in that they both have good arrow-stopping qualities, they can occasionally be treated to prevent their drying out, they cost about the same, and they come in 50-inch, 36-inch, and 24-inch sizes.

The marsh grass targets are round, spirally bound with heavy hemp twine, are about five inches thick, and can be purchased either with or without a burlap covering. The excelsior matts are square, about six inches thick, and consist of paper-covered pads of excelsior tightly compressed and bound with nylon twine and then covered with a sheet of white plastic. Both stand up under hard use but the excelsior matts should be used only indoors because moisture makes the wood expand until it finally breaks the nylon twine. Marsh grass matts can be used either inside or outside, but it is

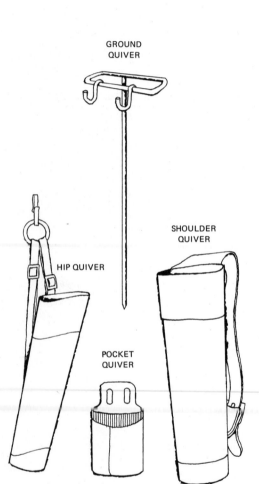

GROUND QUIVER

HIP QUIVER

SHOULDER QUIVER

POCKET QUIVER

Fig. 2-13 Types of quivers.

advisable to use burlap-covered ones indoors to keep any dried grass from getting on the floor.

Some of the indoor archery lanes are using matts made of tightly compressed layers of cardboard, and these have good arrow-stopping qualities. It is also possible on some of them to replace the layers of cardboard as they wear out.

When bales of straw or specially treated excelsior are used for stopping arrows, they are referred to as target "butts." Oversized bales of straw, about 46 inches wide, can be stacked two or three high on a suitable easel, and by rotating the center bales to the top or bottom every eight or nine weeks, a target of three bales can be made to last a full school year. Bales of straw will not stop arrows too well unless they are placed so that the straw shafts are perpendicular to the ground. This places the wires that hold the bales together in such a position that they can be cut by an arrow. If a cut wire is quickly repaired the bale can continue to be used, but if the straw begins to absorb moisture and expand before repairs are made, the bale will have to be discarded. If straw bales are to be used indoors they should be covered with burlap to prevent the dry straw from cluttering the floor.

Excelsior bales, 50 inches wide, are also available for butts. They have been treated to resist moisture and are highly compressed so they stop arrows effectively. They will outlast straw bales but are more expensive. They too must be set on a suitable easel.

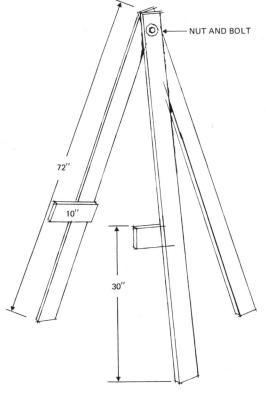

Fig. 2-14 A tripod easel.

Easels

A three-legged or tripod easel made of one-inch by four-inch wood is commonly used for holding the round or square matts (Fig. 2-14). This type of easel can be adjusted so that the target face center is the 51 inches required by the National Archery Association for outdoor tournament shooting. It can also be tilted back to give the necessary slant.

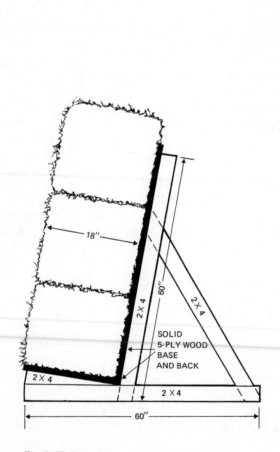

Fig. 2-15 Side view of an easel for a target butt.

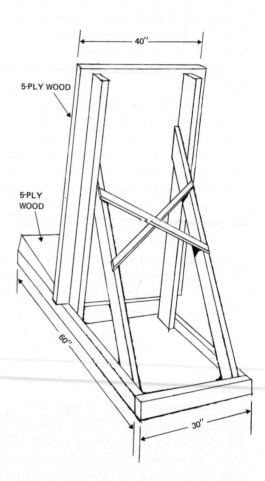

Fig. 2-16 Back view of an easel for a target butt.

For schools and camps the National Archery Association has waived the 51-inch rule, so many of these groups are using a portable easel which somewhat resembles the two-wheeled cart used for carrying golf clubs. This metal target cart has a wider base on which the round or square matt is set and tied. This puts the target face center about 30 inches from the ground. The entire unit is then rolled to and from the range as it is needed, with the matts and faces being left on the cart while it is in storage.

Butts require heavier and bulkier easels because they are about three times as heavy as matts (Figs. 2-15, 2-16). It is therefore more difficult to move them from place to place, so they are found mainly on permanently located outdoor ranges. For use indoors they would need to be placed on rollers similar to the ones put under refrigerators, so that they could be rolled out of the way whenever the space was needed.

Target Faces

Target faces are made of heavy paper, tag board, or toughenized paper and come in 48-inch, 36-inch, 24-inch, 20-inch, 16-inch and 80-centimeter sizes. They are five-colored or a single color, depending on the round for which they will be used. (See Chapter 12.)

The heavy paper faces are used mainly for tournament shooting, where their low cost makes it possible to replace them as often as is needed to continue with accurate scoring. Tag board faces are widely used in indoor archery lane establishments and hold up well under intensive shooting. It is possible to buy extra center pieces which can be glued over the worn area and thus prolong the use of the face. Toughenized faces have a thread running through the paper and this makes the face last much longer. It is also possible, when the face has many holes in the center, to glue a one foot square corner from an old target face to the back of the gold and red circles.

This will make the face usable for a few more days. Toughenized paper faces are used mainly by schools, camps, and recreation departments because they last longer than any of the other kinds.

COSTS OF ARCHERY EQUIPMENT[5]

Bows	Semirecurve, $15-$30
	Working recurve, $30-$200
Bowstrings	Double looped, $1.25-$4.00
Bowsights	$2-$80
Arrows	Wood, $9-$15 per doz.
	Fiberglass, $15-$30 per doz.
	Aluminum, $18-$40 per doz.
Finger protection	Tabs, 25 ¢-$2.50
	Gloves, $1.50-$4.00
Quivers	Hip, $1-$15
	Pocket, $1.50-$5.00
	Shoulder, $16-$25
	Ground, $2-$3.50
Stabilizers	$15-$25
Target matts and Butts	Round marsh grass (48-inch), $32
	Square excelsior (50-inch), $32
	Bales of straw (46-inch), $1.50 per bale, with at least 3 bales needed per butt
	Bales of excelsior, $11 per bale, with at least 3 bales needed per butt

---

5.   1969 retail prices are listed. Schools, camps, and other educational groups are often given a discount by archery dealers.

Easels	Wooden tripod, $7-$9
	Two-wheeled cart, $19-$23
Target faces	16-inch paper, five colors, 20¢
	16-inch corrugated paper, five colors, $19.50 for a pack of 50
	20-inch blue and white chip board, 35¢
	20-inch blue and white corrugated paper, 50¢
	24-inch paper, five colors, 50¢
	24-inch toughenized paper, five colors, 95¢
	36-inch paper, five colors, 95¢
	36-inch toughenized paper, five colors, $1.98
	48-inch paper, five colors, $1.69
	48-inch toughenized paper, five colors, $2.98
	80-cm five colors, $1.00

Second United States Intercollegiate Championships (1969).

safety in target archery

The old saying "An ounce of prevention is worth a pound of cure" was never more true than in archery. There is no such thing as a "toy" bow and arrow. *Every* arrow shot from *any* bow has the potential for injury to people, animals, or property.

Every archer must, at all times, be defensive to prevent injury to himself and alert to prevent injury to others. This involves knowing the potentially dangerous things in archery and then establishing sound safety practices to prevent accidents.

Any sport or life situation is as dangerous as you let it become, but courtesy, cooperation, common sense, and adherence to the established safety rules can make archery as safe and enjoyable a sport as any other.

It is not possible in this book to list *all* the safety precautions that should be enforced in target archery. Each archer, coach, or leader will find that many local safety rules must be established to eliminate dangers found only in his specific situation. However, the following list is a good general summary of major rules that need to be established.

RULES FOR SAFE GENERAL CONDUCT

1. Be safety conscious at all times.
2. Be alert at all times. The archery range is no place for daydreaming, "goofing around," or "horse play."
3. Do not point a nocked arrow at anyone. A nocked arrow is like a loaded gun.
4. Be considerate of others. Use good common sense.
5. Respect your equipment and care for it properly.
6. Never shoot an arrow into the air. There is no way of knowing where, or on whom, it will land.
7. Wear comfortable but appropriate clothing and shoes. Avoid pins, buttons, ruffles, and long or loose-fitting sleeves that could catch the string upon release and cause an accident.
8. Cooperate with the leader in charge of the range. Obey the safety rules and report to him any unsafe practices that are being followed by other archers.
9. Don't take chances. Be a living, walking, talking example of good safety practices in archery.

RULES FOR SAFE CARE AND USE OF EQUIPMENT

1. Check your equipment each day before you use it. Be on the lookout for such things as frayed strings or servings, loose fletchings, nocks or points that are not secure, bent or splintered shafts, or damage to the bow or its attachments.

2. Change frayed strings before they break.

3. Use arrows the correct length (or longer) for you. Never use an arrow that is too short; the danger of injury from an arrow that is overdrawn is great.

4. Never release a string without an arrow on it, since this may damage the limbs of your bow. Practice drawing and anchoring without an arrow and let the string down slowly to its brace-height each time.

5. Always wear an armguard and finger tab (or glove). A sore forearm or finger tips can cause you to make many mistakes in your shooting form. These errors can cause the arrow to travel in unintended directions. A shirt or dress protector may also be a desirable addition since this holds your clothing close to your body and prevents the string, at full-draw, from becoming entangled in it. A protector will also prevent abrasions where the string continually touches the chest at full draw.

6. Before you begin to shoot, be sure there is no one at or behind the target—or between you and the target.

7. Be aware of people. Look where you are going when you are carrying arrows.

8. Carry arrows in your hip, shoulder, or pocket quiver. In the absence of a quiver, put the arrow points in the palm of your hand and spread the arrows out fan-shape, with the nock down so that the fletching is not crushed and the nock cannot push into someone.

9. On the way to the target, watch for arrows embedded in the grass and pick them up. Arrows can be broken and toes injured by running into the nock of an arrow hidden in the grass.

10. When you pick up arrows from the grass use care to prevent injury to the fletching and to archers who are

nearby. If the fletching is embedded in the grass, pull the arrow through the grass, point first, gradually angling it upwards. If the feathers are not caught, pull the arrow out nock first, gradually angling it upwards.

11. Before pulling an arrow from the target, be sure no one is standing in line with its path from the target.

12. When removing arrows from the target, place the back of one hand against the target face and around the arrow. Place the other hand on the arrow as close to the target face as possible. Pull the arrow from the target at the same angle it entered. If the arrow is deeply embedded, twist it a few times to loosen it and then pull it out. Placing one hand against the target makes a target face last longer and saves the embarrassment of pulling the entire target over and breaking the arrows still remaining in it.

13. If any part of the fletching is embedded in the target or target face, go to the back of the target and pull the arrow through point first.

14. If the point of the arrow is embedded in the wood, take hold of the shaft as close to the point as possible and carefully work the arrow back and forth to enlarge the hole and free the point.

RULES FOR SAFETY ON THE RANGE

1. Space archers far enough apart on the shooting line so that they cannot bother or endanger other archers. If the range is small, assign four to six archers to a target and let only half of them shoot at a time, rather than having them crowded dangerously together.

2. Observe the whistle signals. One blast indicates that you should nock the first arrow of an end or that you should

go to the target to retrieve arrows. Two blasts means that there is an emergency somewhere on the range and that you should *immediately* stop shooting. A single short blast will then indicate that the emergency is over and that you may resume shooting.

3. Straddle the shooting line so that no archer is standing slightly ahead of or behind the others.

4. When nocking an arrow, keep the point aimed toward the target.

5. If you drop an arrow in front of the shooting line, pull it back using the tip of your bow. If you cannot reach it, consider it as having been shot and pick it up when the signal to retrieve arrows is given.

6. When you have finished shooting your arrows, step back ten feet from the shooting line so that the official can easily see when all the archers are through. Wait for the signal before you move forward toward the targets.

7. Help your target mates find lost arrows. Do not return to the line without them. Leaving one person hunting for lost arrows may result in his being overlooked and shot at.

8. Do not run with arrows in your hand.

Second United States Intercollegiate Championships (1969).

CHAPTER 4

bracing and unbracing a bow

One of the problems faced by every archer is that of getting his bow braced and ready for shooting. He is concerned with finding a method which, ideally, will meet all of the following criteria:

1. He can use the method easily (it doesn't demand more strength than he has);

2. He can use the method safely (it will not result in injury to him);

3. It will not damage his bow (the method will allow him to brace the bow with *evenly* exerted pressure on the entire width of the bow limb, rather than with pressure near the edge of the limb, which causes a bow limb to twist).

Until recently, there were only two commonly used methods of bracing a bow: the "push-pull" and the "step-through"; but now a device known as a "bow bracer" or "bow stringer" has provided an easier and safer method. Each method will be described and you should try all three. But whichever you decide you prefer, you should always check two things before you begin to brace your bow:

1. The string loop should be securely fastened into the lower notch. The use of a bow-tip protector will ensure this, and at the same time will protect the tip from wear. Another method is to wrap a rubber band over the loop and around the bow several times.

2. The string should not be wrapped around the bow.

HOW TO USE THE PUSH-PULL METHOD

Stand in a side-stride position, toes pointed straight ahead, with your feet farther apart than the width of your hips. Hold your bow with the left hand[1] on the grip, upper limb up, and the back of the bow toward you (Fig. 4-1).

Place the lower tip of the bow on the instep of your left foot, being careful to keep it off the ground. Put your left elbow against your body near your hip bone. This will bring the bow very close to you and straight across the front of your body (Fig. 4-2).

Shift your weight to your left foot and bend your knee forward so that the limb is near the inside of your left calf (Fig. 4-3).

Place your right palm on the back of your bow, just below the loop, so that your thumb is on one side of the bow and your index finger is on the other side. Keep the remaining three fingers straight (Fig. 4-4).

Now look at a spot straight ahead of you. *Do not look at your right hand* (it is dangerous to do so because if your hand slips off the bow, the tip will fly back toward your eyes).

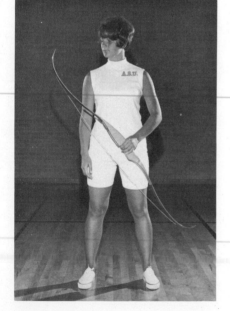

Fig. 4-1 Holding the bow in preparation for bracing it. Note that the feet are pointed straight ahead, so that the bow tip will not slip off during the push-pull process.

1. Some people prefer the right hand and the right foot. Either way is permissible.

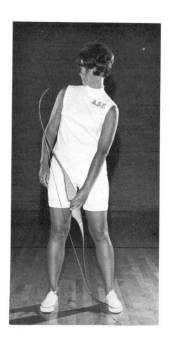

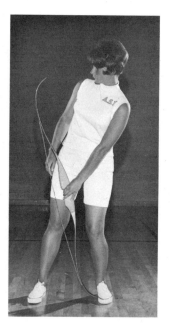

Fig. 4-2 Note that the left elbow is in contact with the hip, so that the bow is brought in close to the body and diagonally across it.

Fig. 4-3 The weight has been shifted to the left foot and the left knee is bent forward; the right leg is straight.

Fig. 4-4 Beginning to push-pull. Note that the archer is not looking at the bow tip and that she has pushed her right shoulder forward. If her right hand now slips off the bow, the tip will hit her in the upper arm instead of the head.

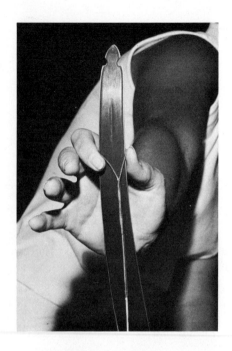

Keeping your body upright, pull with your left hand, and at the same time, thrust your right shoulder forward and push against the back of your bow. Let your right hand slide toward the bow tip and guide the loop toward and into the notch (Fig. 4-5).

When you *feel* the loop slip into the notch, hold onto the string with your right hand, and bring the bow in front of your body, with the string away from you (Fig. 4-6). When the bow is parallel to the ground, look to see if the loop is securely in *both* sides of the notch. If so, take your hand away; if not, replace the bow in bracing position and push-pull until the loop is in its proper place.

Fig. 4-5 Note that the index finger and thumb guide the loop toward the notch, and that the remaining fingers are straight so that they will not be pinched between the string and the face of the bow.

Fig. 4-6 The braced bow has been brought up and forward, but the fingers are still holding the string at the notch. The archer now looks to see whether the loop is in both sides of the notch before letting go of the bow tip.

To unbrace your bow, follow the same procedure, pushing and pulling until the string hangs slack on the bow. Then, with your right index finger, ease the loop out of the notch and let it slide down the limb toward you. Do not look at the bow tip while you unbrace it; it's just as dangerous to do so as it was when you were bracing the bow.

This method, properly followed, has the advantage of causing little or no twist in the bow limb; however, many people find it impossible to do because they do not have sufficient strength or because the push-pull coordination is a difficult one for them to master.

You will note that the archer has been cautioned to look at a spot straight ahead of him as he pushes and pulls. This precaution must be observed because if his hand slips off the bow limb, the tip will snap back toward his head with great force. The forward thrusting of his shoulder during this step is added insurance against being hit in the head by the flying bow tip.

HOW TO USE THE STEP-THROUGH METHOD

Stand in a side-stride position, weight evenly divided, with the inside edges of your feet 20 to 24 inches apart, toes pointed straight ahead. Hold your bow in your right hand[2] about midway between the grip and the upper tip. The back of the bow should be toward you. With your left hand, hold the string about 18 inches from the upper loop, and then pull it away from the bow until it is taut (Fig. 4-7).

Place your right leg and foot between the face of the bow and the string so that the recurved section of the lower limb is in front of your left ankle (Fig. 4-8).

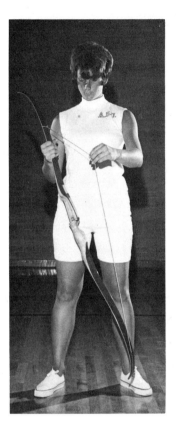

Fig. 4-7 Holding the bow in preparation for stepping between the face and the string.

2.　If you prefer, hold the bow in your left hand and step through with your left foot.

Let go of the string and move your left hand to the upper limb, near the notch. Adjust the bow so that the handle-riser section is high on your right buttocks (or as high on the right thigh as you can get it). Now slide your right hand to a spot just below the loop, with the palm of your hand on the back of the bow and your fingers extended (Fig. 4-9).

Bend the bow by pushing against the back of it with the palm of your right hand, and at the same time, push against the handle-riser section with your buttocks. Guide the string into the upper notch with your left hand (Fig. 4-10).

To unbrace the bow, follow the same procedure, bending the bow until the string hangs slack; then slip it out of the notch with your left hand.

This method seems to be easier for those who lack the necessary strength needed for the push-pull method. However, improper placement of the bow on the left ankle and across the right buttocks can result in pressure on the *edges* of the bow limbs, causing one or both of them to twist. Archers should *quickly* bend the bow and slip the string into the notch; to do this slowly causes prolonged pressure on the front of the left ankle and results in a black and blue mark.

HOW TO USE BOW BRACERS

Although there are several styles of bow bracers available, only two will be mentioned because they all work on the same principles. One style consists of three pieces of wood—a base and two diagonal uprights—which can be set varying distances apart to accommodate bows of different lengths. To use this bracer, adjust it so that the recurved sections of your bow fit into the grooved ends of the diagonal uprights. Place your bow, face up, across the diagonals so that the upper loop of your string is just outside one of them (Fig. 4-11).

Fig. 4-8 The archer has now stepped through with the right foot.

Fig. 4-9 Notice that the handle-riser section is high on the buttocks, and that the four fingers of the right hand are extended.

Fig. 4-10 Pushing against the back of the bow and guiding the loop into the notch.

Move up close to the bow, put one hand on the grip and push straight down, guiding the loop into the notch with the other hand (Fig. 4-12).

To unbrace your bow, follow the same procedure, pushing down until the string is slack; then slip the loop out of the upper notch with your free hand.

Another type of bow bracer consists of a rope, approximately five feet long, having a piece of leather at each end that is shaped so that it will fit snugly over the tips of your bow. Hold your bow face down horizontally in front of you. Place the leather pieces over the tips so that the rope hangs down toward the ground. Put one foot in the center to anchor it (Fig. 4-13).

Pull straight upward on the grip to bend the bow. Guide the loop into the notch with your free hand (Fig. 4-14).

To unbrace the bow, follow the same procedure, bending the bow until the string is slack; then slip the loop out of the upper notch and let it slide down the upper limb.

There are numerous other styles of bow bracers, but all are designed to help you brace your bow more easily and quickly without damage to it or injury to yourself. Every archer who has a bow bracer available should use it, and if he doesn't have this advantage, he should make every effort to get one. In addition, he should master one of the other methods so that he is prepared for any emergency.

Operators of archery lanes have found that composite or fiberglass bows apparently suffer no damage if they are left braced for months at a time. Camp and school instructors might wish to consider leaving their bows braced for the summer or during the instructional unit in school. However, braced bows need a different kind of storage area since they occupy more space. This factor, along with the knowledge that your students would always be dependent upon someone else to brace their bows, may make you decide that they need to learn the skill for themselves.

Fig. 4-11 The bow in position, ready to be braced with the bow bracer.

Fig. 4-12 Bracing the bow.

Fig. 4-13 Ready to use a rope bow bracer.

Fig. 4-14 Guiding the loop into the notch.

Glen Funk, Arizona State University, runner-up 1969 United States Intercollegiate Championships.

target archery technique

Each time an archer shoots an arrow, he must follow an exact pattern of movements which must be repeated in precisely the same way for each succeeding arrow if he wants them to group in the center of the target. So the archer's first objective in learning to successfully shoot a bow and arrow is to gain a thorough understanding of these movements, and his second objective is to make himself correctly perform them.

The technique described in this book is basically that method used by Gilman Keasey[1] in winning the national championship in 1935. His system of shooting has been referred to as the "relaxed method" or the "classic style," but regardless of its name, with slight variations it is the technique still being used by skilled archers today.

To make it easier to learn, the technique of target archery has been divided into nine steps. The order of the steps has

---

1. Natalie Reichart and Gilman Keasey, *Archery,* New York: A.S. Barnes and Company, 1936.

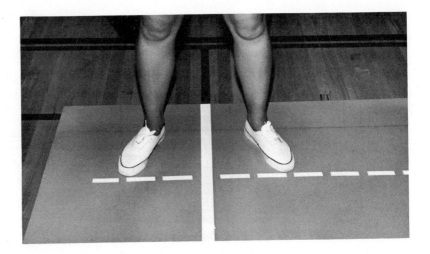

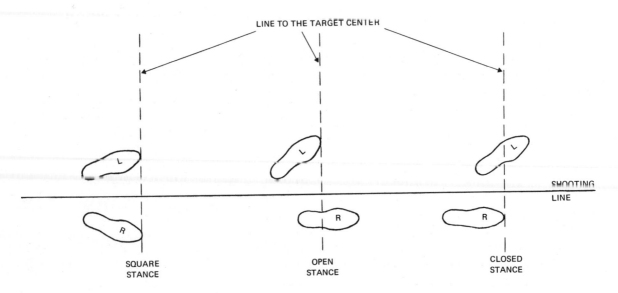

LINE TO THE TARGET CENTER

SHOOTING
LINE

SQUARE
STANCE

OPEN
STANCE

CLOSED
STANCE

Fig. 5-1 Proper foot position straddling the shooting line.

been established through observation and discussion with many of the top target archers and is the logical sequence they follow as they shoot.

STEP 1: BODY POSITION[2]

Straddle the shooting line, assuming a square stance (Fig. 5-1) so that your feet are equidistant from the line on each side of it. The inside edges of your feet should be 12 to 16 inches apart and your weight should be evenly divided. A line drawn from the tip of your right shoe to the tip of your left shoe and extended toward the target should end in the center of the target. Your head should be turned toward the target so that your chin is above your left shoulder and you are looking out toward the target on a line that is parallel to the ground (Fig. 5-2).

Coaching Hints on Body Position

1. Place some kind of marker on the ground or floor to indicate where each foot should be placed. To determine this, lay an arrow across the shooting line so that it points directly to the center of the target at which you will be shooting. Then step up to the line and place one foot properly on each side of it so that the tip of each shoe is just touching the arrow. Pick the arrow up and place a foot marker at the tip of each shoe (or mark the floor with a piece of chalk or tape). Golf tees make simple foot markers for outdoor use. Your feet are now "on the line" to the target; this foot position is known as the "square stance" (Fig. 5-1).

2. The importance of the width of the stance cannot be minimized. If your feet are too close together, it is difficult to

Fig. 5-2 In proper position on the shooting line.

---

2.   All descriptions are for a right-handed archer.

keep good balance during your shooting. If your feet are too far apart, tension develops in the upper legs and this leads to inaccuracies.

3. Although body position is listed as Step 1, you must realize that the details of this technique must be maintained through all the other eight steps.

4. If you have difficulty in getting your head into the proper position, try standing in your place on the shooting line looking at the person standing in front of you. Focus on a spot that is at the level of your eyes; then slowly turn your head and look at the target at which you will be shooting.

5. If you are thick-chested or have husky arms, you may find that a square stance does not allow the string to properly clear your left shoulder, upper arm, or lower arm. If this is the case, try an "open stance" (Fig. 5-1). Move your left foot back far enough so that the line to the target extends from the instep of your right foot to the toes of your left foot. Some archers even move the left foot so far back that the line extends from the heel of their right foot to the toes of their left foot. This open stance moves your left shoulder and arm out of the way of the string when you release it. Avoid a "closed stance" because this rotates your hips, shoulders, and left arm into the path of the string upon release (Fig. 5-1).

STEP 2: HOLDING THE BOW

Using your left hand, circle the grip of the bow so that the knuckle of your index finger and the first joint of your thumb are about equidistant from the ground. The tips of these fingers should lightly overlap each other. The grip of the bow should rest in the palm of your left hand so that the "life line" follows and pushes against the grip near the pivot point. The base of your little finger near your wrist should be just to the

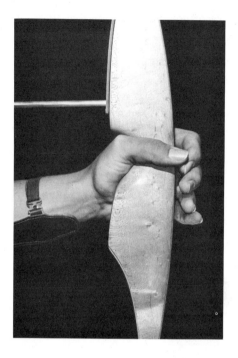

Fig. 5-3 Proper left-hand position on the grip.

left of the grip (Fig. 5-3). The fingers and thumb should exert no pressure on the sides or back of the bow.

Coaching Hints on Holding the Bow

1. Your left hand must be placed in *exactly* the same place on the grip each time you shoot. That spot must be the pivot point so that you are not torquing (turning) the bow, either to the right or to the left, as you release the arrow. To help you get your hand in its same position for every shot, put an inked dot on the upper limb of your bow just above the grip so that it is straight above the pivot point. Now place your hand in its

proper position so that you are pushing against the pivot point toward the center of the target at full-draw. Note the spot on your hand that is directly below the dot on the bow limb and place a dot there. On each shot thereafter, see that these two dots are exactly lined up at full-draw.

2. Avoid gripping the bow. Your left forearm, wrist, hand, and fingers must be as relaxed as is possible throughout the entire shot. Many archers use a wrist sling or a finger sling to keep the bow from dropping to the ground when they release. This makes it possible to keep the fingers of your left hand open and completely relaxed and avoids unnecessary tension in the left hand and arm (Fig. 5-4).

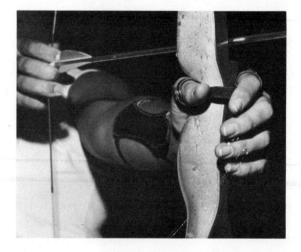

Fig. 5-4 Note the leather finger sling which fits across the back of the bow and is attached to the thumb and index finger.

STEP 3: NOCKING THE ARROW

Hold the bow at your left side parallel to the ground with the palm of your hand facing the ground (Fig. 5-5).

Take hold of an arrow by the nock and lay it on top of the bow so that it is touching the arrow rest and the index feather is extending straight up toward the sky. Slip the nock onto the string just below the nock-locator so that the arrow is approximately one-eighth inch above a perfect right angle. Place your right hand in position (Fig. 5-6) so that the string is precisely in the first joint of the three string fingers. The arrow nock is between your index and middle fingers. There should be very little contact with the arrow and no pressure on it from these two fingers. The fingers should form a right angle with the string. Curl these fingers, but keep the back of your hand flat and relaxed.

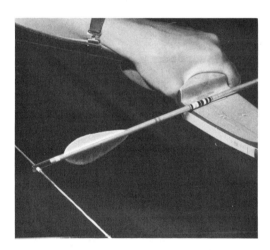

Fig. 5-5 The bow is parallel to the ground and the arrow is properly nocked just below the nock-locator. The index feather is up.

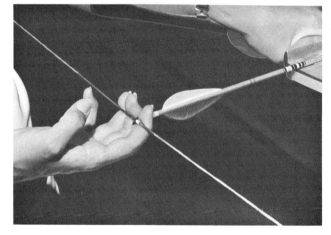

Fig. 5-6 The fingers in position on the string. The archer has purposely discarded her finger tab in order to show how the string should lie in the joint of the three fingers.

Coaching Hints on Nocking the Arrow

1. Each arrow must be nocked in exactly the same spot on the string. The proper nocking point can be determined by shooting in good form at a distance of six feet, using the Hamilton Test.[3] Aim so that your arrows land at the height of your eyes. Shoot several and then look at them from the side. If they land with the nocks higher than the rest of the arrow, your nocking point is too high, and vice versa. Make the needed adjustment until your arrows enter the target parallel to the ground. Mark your nocking point on the string with a pen or pencil; then place a nock-locator of some kind at the proper place so that when you slip your arrow on just below it, the nock is in its correct place on the string.

2. Avoid placing your right thumb in contact with the string. To do so results in tension in your string hand, wrist, and forearm and leads to a scattering of arrows.

3. Before you make the Hamilton test to determine your proper nocking point, measure your brace-height. Make a note of it and thereafter measure it each time you brace your bow. It is important that it always be the same, because if your string stretches, the location of the nocking point has also changed. You are therefore nocking either too low or too high. It is wise to check your brace-height once or twice during a shooting session since a change in it can account for a sudden low or high grouping of your arrows.

STEP 4: THE PREDRAW

Keeping your string fingers in their correct position, move the bow and arrow up and toward the target until your bow is

Fig. 5-7 The predraw position.

3.   Max Hamilton, "Bare Shaft Test," *The Archer's Magazine,* Volume 13, No. 4: April 1964, page 9.

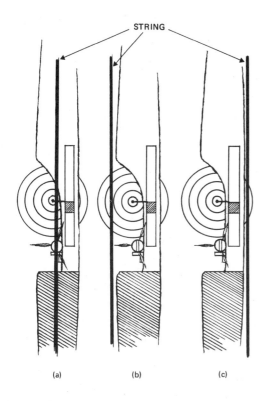

STRING

(a)   (b)   (c)

Fig. 5-8 String patterns. (a) Your head is in the correct position. The string pattern is seen running down the center of the face of the bow during the predraw and aiming steps. (b) Incorrect. Your head is tipped toward the person standing ahead of you on the shooting line. The string pattern is to the left of the bow. (c) Incorrect. Your head is tipped toward the person behind you on the shooting line. The string pattern is to the right of the bow.

perpendicular to the ground and your left arm is straight (Fig. 5-7).

Draw the string back two or three inches so that the grip exerts slight pressure on your bow hand. Relax your left wrist and forearm and check to see that the pivot point is pushing against the correct spot on your bow hand. Look at your string hand to see if the fingers are still at right angles to the string and the back of your hand is flat and relaxed. Close your left eye and move your bow until your bowsight is lined up with the proper aiming spot (see Step 7, Coaching Hints). Now get your head into correct position by moving it until you see the string running down the center of the face of the upper limb (Fig. 5-8a).

You are now looking out of your right eye to the left of the string through the bowsight to the aiming spot on the target. Close your lips and make your back teeth touch; then rotate your left elbow down and out (clockwise). Take a little deeper breath than you usually do, but then expel the *usual* amount. Now hold your breath until after you release the arrow.

Coaching Hints on the Predraw

1. The importance of rotating the left elbow and keeping it rotated cannot be overemphasized. This allows the string to move forward when you release it without hitting your arm and causing a nasty black and blue mark at the elbow. Many archers do not have enough strength in the muscle that does this work and will need to make special efforts to develop it. Try this exercise for the *pronator teres* muscle:

Stand in good shooting position, at arm's length from the narrow edge of a door, as if that were going to be your target. Place your bow hand in position on the narrow edge, at the height of your shoulder. Using the door-edge to stabilize your hand, rotate your left elbow down and out (clockwise) while keeping your left shoulder down and back. Repeat 10 times, holding each trial as long as you can. If you have trouble keeping your shoulder down, have a partner stand behind you and put a hand on top of your left shoulder; you can then *feel* his hand moving as you push your shoulder forward and up.

2. Avoid hunching your shoulders up as you move from the nocking step to the predraw step. Taking the slightly-deeper-than-usual breath and then letting part of it out will help you to relax your shoulders as well as make you steadier during the steps which follow.

3. Some archers are so tense that they have trouble getting the back of their string hand relaxed in this step. Have your

partner stand in front of you and face you on the shooting line; he should then place his index finger on your palm and his thumb on the back of your string hand. With a slight exertion of pressure on your hand, he can make you relax it, and you can then feel the difference between tension and a lack of it in your right hand.

STEP 5: THE DRAW

This step consists of moving the string and the right hand and arm from the predraw position to the anchor position (Step 6). It must be a smooth movement, neither too slow nor too quick. While it is being done, all the details of the preceding steps must continue to be correctly performed.

Begin the draw by using the muscles of your upper right arm, shoulder, and upper back. Your shoulders must be kept down and the shoulderblades squeezed together behind you. Your right elbow moves back from the very beginning of the draw and should be up and at the same height as your arrow. When you reach your anchor spot, there should be a straight line from the tip of your arrow to the tip of your right elbow. If you turned your hips off the line to the target during the predraw, you must bring them back to the line as you draw the string back in this step, so that your feet, hips, and shoulders are again on the line to the target. The draw ends when the string is touching the center of your chin and the tip of your nose and your string hand is in its correct anchor spot (Fig. 5-9).

Coaching Hints on the Draw

1. Hold your head in its proper position and draw the string to your head rather than allowing your head and chin to reach out to meet the string as it approaches.

Fig. 5-9 Note that the string touches the tip of the nose and the center of the chin, while the index finger is under the jawbone.

2. Avoid pulling the string back solely through the use of your upper-arm muscles. Begin the draw by pulling your shoulderblades together and then maintain this tension until after the arrow hits the target.

3. From the very instant you begin to draw the string back, you must keep the bow arm, hand, and fingers relaxed. You will feel the *push* of the bow against your hand and on up your left arm into your shoulder. Since your left elbow is locked and rotated out of the way, and since your shoulders are down and being squeezed together behind you, everything the bow is pushing against is firm and steady. Keep it that way! Don't try to push the bow. The *bow* does the pushing and all you do is give it something immoveable to push against.

4. The three fingers of your string hand act as dead hooks on the string. Get them curled around the string and then avoid squeezing them in toward the palm of your hand any further. To do so will cause the arrow to fall off the arrow rest during the draw, anchor, and aiming steps.

STEP 6: THE ANCHOR

The top edge of your right index finger must be placed firmly in contact with a precise and definite spot under your jawbone so that the arrow nock is directly below your nose. This is your "anchor spot." Your right thumb and little finger must remain relaxed and the thumb will rest somewhere near your Adam's apple on your neck. The string should be firmly touching the tip of your nose and the center of your chin. Keep your lips together and back teeth touching (Fig. 5-10).

Coaching Hints on the Anchor

1. The anchor must have a feeling of being the same on every shot. Your index finger must be in the same spot so that

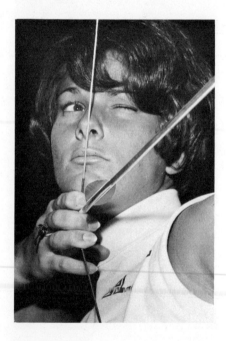

Fig. 5-10 The anchor. Note that the thumb is relaxed and well below the jaw near the neck.

the nock of the arrow is in the same place. The string must touch the tip of your nose every time or you may have the nock higher from the ground on those shots where it is not touching. It must have the same feeling of firmness, because a light anchor doesn't steady the nock of the arrow to the same degree as a firm anchor.

2. It is important to relax the back of your string hand *and* the thumb and little finger to reduce unnecessary tension. A tense thumb makes it very difficult to get your index finger under your jawbone.

3. The tension between your shoulderblades must be evenly maintained during this step. To ease up on it the least bit will allow the point of the arrow to creep forward while you are aiming (Step 7) and will cause the arrow to drop low.

4. If you cannot get the feel of putting your right index finger under your jawbone, have a partner stand in front of you on the shooting line, facing you, during the predraw. He should place his right index finger on top of and across your right index finger, at right angles to it. Now, while you draw, he should keep his index finger on yours so that when you get to the anchor spot you can feel his finger under your jaw. He should then slip his finger out of the way and you will be anchored in the proper place.

STEP 7: HOLDING AND AIMING

The most accurate method of aiming is with the use of a bowsight. If you are not familiar with the principles of using one, pause for a moment and read the first coaching hint below.

The term "holding" refers to maintaining every detail of correct technique thus far described until the act of "aiming" can be completed. Assuming that you are "holding" in perfect form, allow yourself time to settle down so that your bowsight appears to be perfectly still on the proper aiming spot on the target face. Then check the blur of the string in front of your eyes to see if you have moved your head or are not anchored in the proper place. If everything is in order, the string should still bisect the face of your bow. If the string pattern has moved to the right or left (Fig. 5-8b, c), move your head or your string hand on the anchor spot until it does appear correct. Now, once more check to be sure that your bowsight is resting steady on the aiming spot and when it is, you are ready for the next step.

Coaching Hints on Holding and Aiming

1. The main kinds of bowsights are explained in Chapter 2; all of them work on the same principles:

a) The bowsight aims the point of your arrow, both vertically and horizontally.

b) The exact position of the bowsight on the sight strip, for any given yardage, must be determined by each archer through trial and error. The closer you are to the target, the higher on the strip your bowsight will be; the farther you are, the lower it will be.

c) If your arrows are grouping high on the target, move your bowsight higher; if they are grouping too low, move it lower; if they are to the right, move it to the right; and if they are to the left, move it to the left.

d) If you are using a pin, peep, or cross-hair bowsight, line up the pinhead, hole, or crossed hairs with the exact center of the gold. The bottom of the post sight is generally lined up with a spot where the gold and red scoring circles touch each other at what would be 6 o'clock (or 12 o'clock) on the face of a clock.

2. To help get your bowsight on precisely the right spot, imagine that there is a hummingbird sitting at the proper aiming spot and that your bowsight must be lined up *exactly* with the pupil in his eye.

3. Holding your bowsight steady on the aiming spot is important for accuracy. This ability is closely related to acquiring the necessary strength and endurance in your arm, back, and shoulder muscles. See Chapter 10 for exercises that are appropriate. Practice "holding" at full-draw for as long as possible, working up to at least 45 seconds.

4. Aiming cannot be done quickly. A minimum of five seconds is required and skilled archers have been timed for 13 seconds!

5. No method of aiming will be effective until you have developed consistency in your shooting form, so practice good form. It takes 10 good shots to counteract one bad shot.

6. When checking your string pattern in this step, the string will no longer look sharp and clear as it did in the predraw step. It will appear as a blur in front of your face because it is now so close to your eye. You should, however, still see the blur bisecting the upper limb.

STEP 8: RELEASING

In this step, continue to do everything that you have been doing up to this instant, with one exception: simply, easily, and smoothly allow your string fingers to relax—just let them become limp. When this has been done, the string will roll gently off your fingertips. As it does, it will straighten your fingers enough so that it can make a smooth "get-away" (avoid *forcing* your fingers to straighten out—let the string do that job when you relax them).

Because the tension between your shoulderblades is still being kept, your right hand and arm will automatically move back and away from the target and will, as a reaction to the force of the string leaving the fingers, slide along underneath your jawbone until your shoulderblades have met. This is a *reaction* rather than a movement which you make yourself do (Fig. 5-11).

During the release, your left hand must remain relaxed and all other details of technique must remain as they were before the release.

Coaching Hints on the Release

1. Make your release as smooth as possible. Avoid forcing your fingers to open; let the string do this job as it moves forward.

2. Continue to pull your shoulderblades together so that your right hand will recoil of its own accord as soon as you relax your three string fingers.

3. If you find yourself grabbing the bow, try using a wrist sling or a finger sling (Fig. 5-4). Either of these devices will prevent the bow from falling when you release, so that you can keep your left hand relaxed. This common mistake of grabbing your bow can make your arrows scatter on the target face.

4. Avoid allowing your shoulders to collapse as you release. This causes your arrow to drop low because the bow is moving down as the arrow clears it. Continue to pull your shoulderblades together until *after* you hear the arrow hit the target.

5. Avoid trying to see your arrows in flight. Listen for the arrow hitting the target. The only arrows you should see landing are those that hit on your aiming spot. There is an old saying in archery: "You look up to see an arrow landing high

Fig. 5-11 The follow-through. Note that the bow hand is still relaxed and that the string hand has moved back and is also relaxed.

on the target." (In other words, without your realizing it you have raised your bow hand and the bow and sight a slight amount as you looked up. Your bowsight is no longer lined up with the gold, but with a spot higher up.)

STEP 9: FOLLOWING THROUGH

After relaxing the fingers of your string hand and allowing the string to move forward, hold your shooting position for four or five seconds (Fig. 5-12). This is the *follow-through* and it serves two main purposes:

1. Knowing that you are going to hold your shooting position for four or five seconds makes you less apt to allow your shoulders to collapse as you release.

2. It gives you the necessary time and opportunity to check for possible errors in your shooting form so that you will not repeat them on the next arrow:

a) Your left eye should still be closed and the right eye still focused on the proper aiming spot.

b) You should still be squeezing your shoulderblades together.

c) Your bow hand and arm should still be up and in line with the gold on the target face.

d) Your right hand should still be in contact with and under your jawbone, fingers relaxed, and palm facing in toward your neck.

These four things can be easily checked in four or five seconds if you train yourself to do it. After having determined which of these errors you made, lower your arms to your side and rest your finger, hand, arm, shoulder, and back muscles. Use these 10 or 12 seconds to concentrate on perfectly performing the next shot.

Fig. 5-12 Note that the arrow has hit the target and that the archer is still holding her follow-through position.

Coaching Hints on the Follow-Through

1. This is the most frequently ignored of the nine steps and yet it has the greatest potential for helping you increase your skill. Until you can detect your mistakes, it is not possible to correct them, and until they are corrected, you have little chance of grouping your arrows in the center of the target.

2. Skilled archers "dry shoot" (they mentally shoot an arrow in perfect form, step-by-step) as they rest after shooting each arrow. They thereby maintain their concentration on perfect technique, and this mental practice is a positive aid in shooting the next arrow in perfect form.

Every archer must realize that mentally mastering each of the preceding details is not enough. It is one thing to *know* what you want to do, but it is often quite difficult to make yourself do it that way. It is also true that unless you know what you want to do, you can't make yourself do it.

Therefore, your first job is to learn what you must make yourself do with your bow and arrow so that you have a clear mental picture of all the details and the sequence in which they should be done. Then, to achieve the next goal—translating this knowledge into action—requires great concentration. Once you take your position on the shooting line in Step 1, no other thoughts must enter your mind. You must think solely about the proper execution of each detail and in what sequence the details should be checked. You should be concentrating on this task to such a degree that you are not aware of people, noises, or other distracting elements. Your whole being must be tuned to shooting one arrow at a time, and shooting it perfectly. *This is your ultimate and single goal!* When your first arrow has been shot, you must determine by analysis what mistakes you made, resolve to correct them, and then forget the first arrow in favor of concentrating completely on shooting the *next* one flawlessly. Shoot it as if it were the only one you would shoot all day.

You would do well to adopt the slogan "Shoot for form and good scores will follow." Improvement in form will lead to greater consistency, which in turn leads to better grouping on the target and thus to higher scores.

The historic First United States Intercollegiate Championships, 1967, Tempe, Arizona.

CHAPTER 6

the use of a checklist for shooting form

In Chapter 5 we stressed the fact that you cannot successfully shoot even one arrow without consciously and methodically *thinking* about every detail of the technique. The human mind cannot remain a blank for more than a few seconds, and if you are not thinking about your shooting form, you will be thinking about something else. For example, if you are thinking, as you take your bow in hand and step up to the shooting line, "That surely was a good show last night," you can rest assured that your score for that end will not be up to its usual standard.

It is absolutely essential that all your thoughts be concentrated on one thing, and that one thing alone: *shoot this one arrow perfectly.* Forget the last arrow you shot; it's already gone and there is nothing you can do about changing where it landed. All you can do is learn from it what you did wrong, and resolve not to repeat that mistake on the next arrow. Attempt to shoot every arrow in perfect form; this will give you the high scores you are seeking.

If you agree that shooting for form is the best way to raise your scores, there are several facts you should keep in mind:

1. You must know the details of good shooting form.
2. You must be aware of your own deviations from good form.
3. You must concentrate on each of the nine steps in its proper order. It is not possible to successfully shoot an arrow if you think about "aiming" while you are in the "nocking" step.

Discussions with top target archers indicate that each has established a personal routine of checking the details of his shooting form and that this routine is followed in *precisely the same order for each arrow.* This "grooves" your thinking and makes it easier to concentrate on the list of things which you need to check.

No two archers will have precisely the same checklist, since each has his own weaknesses and knows precisely the things he must watch for as he prepares to release an arrow. A beginner's checklist would look quite different from that of a highly skilled archer, but it is possible to set up a general list of details and then allow each person to add or drop items to fit his own problems. Here's how it might look:

Step 1: Body Position

Feet in the same spot.
Weight evenly distributed.

Step 2: Holding the Bow

Bow hand in exactly the same spot each time.
Fingers and wrist relaxed.

Step 3: Nocking

Arrow nocked correctly.
String fingers properly placed on the string.
Back of the hand and wrist relaxed and flat.

Step 4: Predraw

Bow perpendicular to the ground.
Pressure of the bow on the hand in the proper spot.
Bow arm, wrist, and fingers relaxed.
Left eye closed.
String pattern correct.
Bowsight lined up with the target center.
Left elbow rotated.
Teeth together, lips closed.

Step 5: Drawing

Squeeze the shoulderblades together.
Keep the left shoulder down and back.
The hips and shoulders come back on to the line to the target.

Step 6: Anchoring

Right index finger under the jawbone.
String touching the tip of the nose and center of the chin.

Step 7: Holding and Aiming

Tension between the shoulderblades still maintained.
String pattern still correct.
Sight steady and on the proper aiming spot.

Step 8: Releasing

Relax fingers of the string hand.
Maintain tension between shoulderblades.

Step 9: Following Through

Aiming eye still focused on the target.

Left eye still closed.

Tension between the shoulderblades still maintained.

Bow arm still up and fingers relaxed.

Right hand in its proper position and fingers relaxed.

Resting Period

Concentrate on overcoming the mistakes you made on the last shot, and prepare for the next shot.

The use of a checklist not only helps you concentrate on what you are doing but it also makes it easier to determine where and when you made a slight change in your shooting form. This is especially useful in tournament shooting when, under the pressure of competition, you suddenly develop an unusual fault, such as shooting high right on the target. If you know what causes arrows to group high and to the right, it is simple, by a process of elimination as you work through your checklist, to determine what changes in your form suddenly gave you this problem. This restores your confidence and you are back in your "groove" again. The archer who has an automatic form cannot make this discovery and is at a great disadvantage when he develops a shooting error. He loses confidence because he can't discover what he is doing wrong, and therefore cannot correct it.

So establish your personal checklist. Include in it the items that you are most apt to make mistakes on; then memorize it and practice using it until you almost automatically check off those items for each arrow shot. Be sure, however, that you are consciously thinking about the checklist items, because if you are not, you'll find yourself thinking about something else as you try to shoot.

Rose Svarc, San Bernardino Valley College, fourth place; Sue Loftis, University of Arizona, 1969 Champion; Kirstie Kaiser, Arizona State University, third place.

CHAPTER 7

how an arrow flies: the archer's paradox

The way an arrow behaves when the string is released by the archer was, for many years, a confusing contradiction of ideas. It was not until 1941, when Dr. C. N. Hickman filmed his ultraslow motion pictures of an arrow upon its release and during its flight, that much of the speculation concerning arrow behavior was replaced with facts. His films showed how an arrow bends upon release, and how it clears the bow on its way to the target. They explained, for the first time, the phenomenon known as "The archer's paradox."

Webster defines the word "paradox" as: "An assertion that contradicts common sense, but that yet may be true in fact." The characteristics of an arrow in flight are indeed paradoxical; they do not make sense but are nevertheless true.

If you are not shooting a true center shot bow, the point of your arrow at full-draw is somewhere between one-eighth and one-half inch to the left of the line to the target, while the nock is on that line (Fig. 7-1). Logically, it would seem that the arrow should always land to the left of the target center,

LINE TO
THE TARGET

BOW

Fig. 7-1 The Archer's Paradox.

since it is angled off in that direction. But the fact is, it will land in the center of the target—and that is the "archer's paradox." The explanation for this fact lies in what happens to the arrow when it is released and how it then travels to the target.

To better understand the actions of your arrow, it is first necessary to visualize the movements of the bowstring.[1] The string upon release moves slightly to the left, somewhere between one-half and one inch because it must roll off your finger tips and clear your finger tab. A law of motion states: "For every action there is an equal and opposite reaction." Obeying this law of motion, having first moved one-half inch to the left, your string now moves one-half inch to the right, and then a lesser distance left when it has moved forward to about brace-height on your bow. Because the string is attached to the bow tips, it can only move forward a limited distance, and having reached this limit, it immediately reverses itself an equal amount to the right of center as it comes back to brace-height with a slight vibrating action (Fig. 7-2).

At the instant of release, the string rolls slightly to the left, and the arrow nock moves with it (Fig. 7-3). At this same moment, the full force of the draw-weight of your bow is transferred to your arrow in one hard thrust. Thus, in a fraction of a second, 20 or more pounds of force is transferred to the inert arrow.

The arrow point at release is resting against the arrow plate. When the nock moves left to clear your finger tab and the thrust of the draw-weight is transferred to the arrow at the instant of release, the arrow point is made to push toward the right and against the arrow plate because it is following the "equal and opposite reaction" law. The bow resists this push, causing the arrow to bend to the right of the line to the target.

---

1.   Bill Webb, "Arrows Bend Around The Bow," *Archery World,* Volume 15, No. 5; May 1966, page 10.

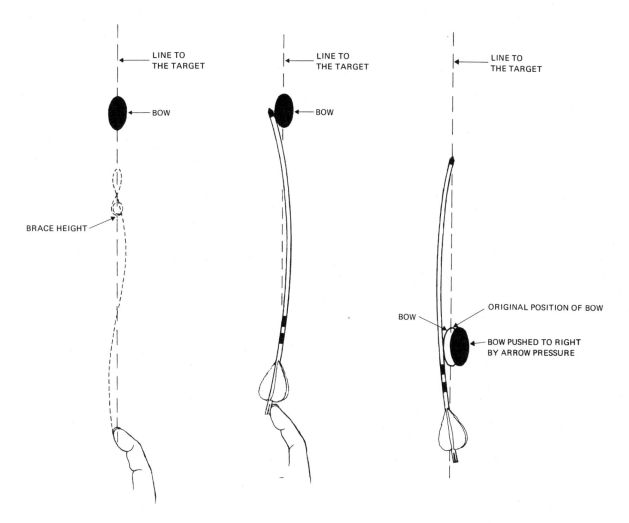

LINE TO
THE TARGET

BOW

BRACE HEIGHT

LINE TO
THE TARGET

BOW

LINE TO
THE TARGET

ORIGINAL POSITION OF BOW

BOW

BOW PUSHED TO RIGHT
BY ARROW PRESSURE

Fig. 7-2 The action of the string after release.

Fig. 7-3 The action of the arrow at the instant of release.

Fig. 7-4 How the arrow clears the bow.

How an Arrow Flies: The Archer's Paradox   75

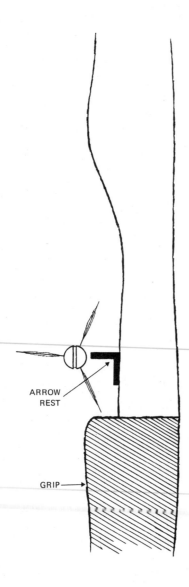

Fig. 7-5 How the arrow passes the bow.

ARROW
REST

GRIP →

As the arrow point pushes against the bow with the force of the draw-weight behind it, it pushes the bow slightly to the right (Fig. 7-4). Meanwhile, the arrow, following the "equal and opposite reaction" law, has bent to the left. These two combined factors make it possible for the arrow to bend around the bow without touching it. (Fig. 7-5). Having cleared the bow, the arrow continues on its way to the target, alternately bending right and left in diminishing amounts (Fig. 7-6). When it is about 10 feet in front of the bow, it will no longer be bending and will be on the line to the target.

The necessary and *proper* bending of your arrow upon release becomes the reason why your arrow, angled off to the left at full-draw, will land in the center of the target. It must bend just enough to clear the bow and come back precisely on the line to the target. It therefore becomes necessary for you to use an arrow which will bend exactly the right amount with the thrust of your draw-weight behind it at release. Such an arrow is said to be "matched to your bow."

The amount an arrow will bend is known as its "spine." An arrow which will bend easily has more spine than one which is stiff.

With wooden arrows of any given length and diameter, it is very difficult to find six arrows that have the same spine because of differences in the grain, density, and weight of the wood. Fiberglass and aluminum arrows are easier to match because they are machine manufactured products and their quality can be more closely controlled. Since aluminum arrows are the more accurate-shooting of the two, we shall discuss them, however, most of what we say also applies to fiberglass arrows.

There are three factors which determine the spine of an aluminum arrow: its length, its diameter, and the thickness of the walls of the aluminum tubing. If the second and third factors are the same, a long arrow will have more spine than a short one; if factors one and three are the same, a thin arrow will have more spine than a thick one; if factors one and two are the same, a thin-walled tube will have more spine than a thick-walled one.

If an arrow has too much spine, it will bend too much upon release and will clear the bow by more space than it should. It will therefore move farther to the right on its next bend and will not be able to get back on the line to the target. It will usually travel on a line to the right of the target center and land to the right. However, arrows with too much spine for the bow from which they were shot have been known to scatter widely on the target, due, no doubt, to their limberness and erratic flight.

If an arrow is so stiff that it does not bend enough upon release, it will not clear the bow properly. In fact, it often hits the bow so hard that you can hear its clatter. Because of its lack of sufficient initial bend, the arrow, on its second bend, assumes a line of travel to the left of the line to the target. If it hits the bow on the way by, it will be thrust even further left and land to the left of the center of the target.

How then do you find the correct combination of length, diameter, and wall thickness to match your bow? Any archery dealer can supply you with a chart which will tell you what size aluminum arrow you need for a particular draw-weight. These charts have been developed by the manufacturer and each takes into account the three factors which affect the spine of an arrow. You therefore get an arrow which bends just the right amount for your draw-weight and which clears the bow properly to give more accurate results.

A further discussion of the problem of matching arrows to your bow will be found in Chapter 9.

LINE TO
THE TARGET

BOW

Fig. 7-6 How the arrow travels to the target.

The 1969 United States Intercollegiate "long line of white." All (90) contestants in white

CHAPTER 8

common shooting problems
and how to correct them[1]

Problem 1: Your Arrow Falls off the Arrow Rest

Caused By   *Solutions*

A. Pinching the nock between your fingers.   Move your index finger a very short distance
                                                away from the nock.

                                                Trim off some of the finger tab if the slit is
                                                not wide enough to accommodate the nock.

B. Increasing the muscular tension in your   Keep the back of your right hand, thumb,
    string fingers.   little finger, wrist, and forearm relaxed.

                                                Start the draw by squeezing your shoulder-
                                                blades together.

C. Drawing the string out and away from   Make your right hand move straight back,
    your left arm.   keeping the string close to your left arm as
                                                you draw.

---

1. All problems, causes, and solutions are discussed for a right-handed archer.

Problem 2: Your Left Shoulder is Hit by the String

Caused By

A. Hunching your left shoulder forward and up during the draw.

B. A closed stance.

C. Pulling the upper part of your body upward during the predraw or draw.

Solutions

Begin the draw by squeezing your shoulder-blades together; maintain this tension until after the arrow hits the target.

Use a lighter weight bow until you can exercise the upper back, shoulder, and arm muscles enough to gain the necessary strength. See Chapter 10.

Check to see that you have a square stance (Chapter 5, Step 1).

Slump a little at the waist. Get the feeling that you are settling your body weight down onto your feet before you start the draw.

Problem 3: Your Left Elbow, Forearm, and/or Wrist Are Hit by the String

Caused By

A. Your elbow not being in its rotated position at the instant of release.

B. Your bow hand being too far inside the string.

C. Your bow becoming understrung.

Solutions

Rotate your elbow clockwise during the predraw and keep it rotated until after the arrow hits the target.

Use a slightly shorter arrow so that you do not try to extend your draw.

Check your bow hand position to see that the base of your little finger is just *to the left side of the bow grip.*

Place your left hand in its proper position so that the pivot point of the bow is pushing against your life line, rather than against the right side of the grip.

Shorten the bowstring until it is the proper distance from the pivot point when the bow is braced.

Problem 4: The Fingers of Your String Hand Become Sore

Caused By

A. Raising your right elbow on the draw or anchor, thus forcing the inside edge of your index finger down onto the nock and creating a sore spot next to your finger nail.

B. The friction of the string as it rolls off your finger tips, an uneven string tension on your fingers, or a finger tab which is too short.

C. Turning your right palm toward the ground during the release, thus allowing the string to roll off one finger after the other, rather than simultaneously.

Solutions

Move your index finger a very short distance away from the nock.

Place the string a little *back* of the joint of your ring finger so that this finger must do a little more of the work on the draw and anchor steps.

A high right elbow is almost always the result of a lazy ring finger. Concentrate on feeling the string pressure on *that* finger just as much as on the other two.

Toughen the skin of your string fingers by periodically painting them with tincture of benzoin.

The use of a good, well-fitted finger tab is a must.

In the nocking step, check to see that the string fingers are all properly placed on the string, and then recheck their position in the predraw.

At the start of the draw, make sure that all three fingers are receiving even pressure from the string. Recheck this during the anchor step.

Avoid using the muscles of your right forearm and wrist on the release. Simply *relax* the string fingers.

Problem 5: Your Arrow Wobbles in Flight

Caused By

A. The string touching your body, arm-guard, or clothing before the arrow has left contact with the string.

B. Nocking your arrow too high or too low.

C. A poor right-hand release.

D. Need for adjustment of the pressure point on the arrow plate.

Solutions

Pull your left shoulder down and back (see Problem 2).

Wear a tight-sleeved garment.

Place two or three rubber bands around your arm to hold the sleeve tight against the arm. Be sure the left elbow is rotated (see Problem 3A). Be sure your left hand is in its proper position on the bow handle (see Problem 3B).

See Chapter 5, Step 3, to determine where to properly nock the arrow.

Concentrate on simply *relaxing* your string fingers as you release. Let the string roll gently off the tips of your fingers. Keep the right palm facing in (toward the neck).

Test your tackle tune-up by doing the variation of the Hamilton Bare Shaft Test (Chapter 9).

Problem 6: Your Arrows Group to the Right

Caused By

A. A wind blowing from left to right.

B. An incorrect bowsight setting.

C. Canting or tipping the top of your bow to the right.

Solutions

Move your bowsight to the right.

Move your bowsight to the right.

Get your bow perpendicular to the ground during the predraw step.

Check during the aiming step to see that the string cuts the center of the face of the bow.

Caused By	*Solutions*
	Avoid allowing your weight to shift toward your toes.
	Avoid leaning forward from your waist during the draw, anchor, and aiming steps.
D. Throwing your string fingers out and away from your jaw during the release (plucking).	Concentrate on simply *relaxing* your string fingers.
E. Changing your string pattern to the left side of the center of the face of the bow.	Tip your head a little more toward the person behind you on the shooting line, and *then* line the string up *exactly* in the center of your nose and chin. See Chapter 5, Step 4, for the proper string pattern.
F. Placing your bow hand too far to the left on your bow grip, thus putting a clockwise torque on the bow.	Carefully place the bow hand in its proper position and then use the "two-dot" system (Chapter 5, Step 2) to get the proper bow hand position. Push on the pivot point of the bow rather than on the left side of it.
G. Pushing or throwing your bow hand to the right as you release.	Keep your bow hand and fingers relaxed until after the arrow hits the target.
	Hunching your left shoulder (Problem 2) can also be a reason for this problem.
	Keep your bow arm and hand relaxed. Avoid trying to follow the flight of the arrow. Keep aiming until after the arrow hits the target.
	Use a wrist or finger sling so that the bow hand may stay completely relaxed until after the arrow hits the target.
H. Moving your string hand in toward your Adam's apple as you release.	Avoid *forcing* your fingers to open on the release. Relax them and let the string roll off your fingertips.

Caused By	Solutions
I. Peeking to see where your arrow has gone.	Make your release as smooth and relaxed as possible. Avoid moving your head to watch the arrow in flight. Keep your eyes on the proper aiming spot.
J. Using arrows too weakly spined for the bow.	Use the same arrows with a lighter bow; or Use stiffer arrows with the same bow. The spine of the arrow should be matched to the bow. Consult an arrow-spining chart.
K. Holding the string too far in on your string fingers.	Carefully place the string *in the first joint* of all three string fingers during the nocking step.
L. Lining up your feet, hips, and/or shoulders to the right of the line to the target.	Recheck the placement of your foot markers. Take a little wider stance to give you better balance (Chapter 5, Step 5).

Problem 7: Your Arrows Group to the Left

Caused By	Solutions
A. A wind blowing from right to left.	Move your bowsight to the left.
B. An incorrect bowsight setting.	Move your bowsight to the left.
C. Tipping the top of your bow to the left during the aiming step.	Get the bow perpendicular to the ground during the predraw. Check to see during aiming that the string still cuts the center of the face of the bow and that your weight has not shifted toward your heels.

Caused By	*Solutions*
D. Moving your string pattern to the right.	Tip your head a little more toward the person in front of you on the shooting line and then realign the string *exactly* in the center of your chin and *exactly* on the tip of your nose.
E. Placing your bow hand too far to the right, thus putting a counterclockwise torque on the bow.	Carefully place your bow hand in its proper position and then use the "two-dot" system (Chapter 5, Step 2) to get your bow hand properly placed thereafter. Push on the *center* of the pivot point of the bow rather than on the right side.
F. Hitting your left shoulder, elbow, shirt sleeve, or armguard.	See Problems 2 and 3. Wear a tight-sleeved shirt.
G. Gripping your bow tightly.	Keep your left thumb and index finger lightly touching around the bow so that it will not jump out of your hand on the release.
	Avoid tension in your left hand, wrist, and forearm.
	The correct use of a finger or wrist sling will also remedy this mistake.
H. Flinching as you release.	Be sure your left elbow is properly rotated so that the elbow cannot possibly be hit by the string.
	Wear an armguard at all times.
I. Pinching the nock of your arrow.	See Problem 1.
J. Pulling the string with your fingers.	See Problem 1.
K. Aiming with your left eye.	Close your left eye and aim with your right eye.
	Wear an eye patch over your left eye.

Caused By	*Solutions*
L. Anchoring to the right of the usual anchor spot under the jaw (or anchoring at the side of the jaw instead of under it).	Have a partner check to see if your index finger is being brought to *exactly* the same spot on every shot. Changing the anchor spot will also change the pattern of the string down the center of the face of the bow.
M. Using arrows that are too stiffly spined for your bow.	Use the same arrows with a heavier bow; or Use weaker-spined arrows with the same bow. The spine of the arrow should be matched to your bow. Consult an arrow-spining chart.
N. Having the index feather *down* in the nocking step.	Be sure, during Step 3, that the index feather is pointed *up* to the roof (or sky).
O. Lining up your feet, hips, and/or shoulders to the left side of the target.	Check to see that your feet are on the line to the target and that your weight is not on your heels. Take a little wider stance to give better balance. See Chapter 5, Step 1.

Problem 8: Your Arrows Group Too High

Caused By	*Solutions*
A. A strong tail wind	Move the bowsight up.
B. An incorrect bowsight setting.	Move the bowsight up.
C. Opening your mouth, thus lowering the anchor spot.	Keep your lips together and your teeth touching. Don't chew while shooting.
D. Lifting your nose from the string.	Feel the string *firmly* touching the tip of your nose and the center of your chin. Keep your shoulders down and back.

Caused By	Solutions

E. Extending your bow arm more than usual.

Get a feeling of "sameness" on every shot.

Use a slightly shorter arrow to avoid having to stretch to get the arrow all the way back.

F. Nocking the arrow too low.

Find the proper nocking point and mark it on the string (Chapter 5, Step 3).

G. Raising your bow arm and hand at the instant of release.

Don't try to follow the flight of the arrow.

Emphasize the follow-through step. Keep pushing your left hand toward the gold and keep aiming during the follow-through.

Check the position of your bow arm and keep the bowsight on a level with the gold in the follow-through.

H. Releasing while your bowsight is still above the proper aiming spot.

Hold long enough to be sure you are lined up and holding *steady* on the proper aiming spot in the gold.

I. The top string finger not being on the string or not taking as much string pressure as the other two. (A lazy middle finger can also cause this problem.)

Carefully place the string *in the joint* of *all three* fingers during predraw and then check the evenness of the string pulling against them during the draw and anchor.

Keep your *right* arm at shoulder level.

J. Anchoring farther back than usual.

Work for a consistent anchor spot.

K. Lowering the anchor.

Work for a consistent anchor spot and *feel* your index finger touching under your jawbone. Keep your teeth and lips together.

L. Leaning away from the target.

Keep your weight evenly divided on both feet. Avoid leaning away from the target at the waist.

M. Snapping your right hand *down* as you release.

Avoid using the muscles of the right wrist and forearm as you release.

Caused By	*Solutions*
	Work for a smooth, relaxed release which will allow your hand to slide *backward along your jawbone.*
N. Heeling the bow.	During the draw and anchor steps, check for a feeling of the bow pushing against the proper spot on your left hand.

Problem 9: Your Arrows Group Too Low

Caused By	*Solutions*
A. A strong headwind.	Move your bowsight down.
B. An incorrect bowsight setting.	Move your bowsight down.
C. Shooting a bow which is understrung.	Shorten the string until it is the proper distance from the pivot point when it is braced.
D. Placing your left hand higher on the grip than usual or raising the base of your thumb off the grip (shooting with your left wrist straight).	Take special care when taking hold of your bow, and check during the draw and anchor steps, to see that the bow is always pushing against the same spot on your left hand.
	Relax your bow hand and arm as much as possible.
E. An incomplete draw (the string is not touching your nose and chin).	Bring the string back until it pulls into the tip of your nose and chin.
F. Creeping.	Keep your right hand *firmly* on the anchor spot.
	Continue to squeeze your shoulderblades together until *after* the arrow hits the target.
	Rotate your left elbow without bending it.
	Exercise your back and shoulder muscles to strengthen them (Chapter 10).

Caused By	*Solutions*
G. Dropping your bow hand during the release step.	Keep aiming during the follow-through. Don't peek to see your arrows in flight. Keep tension between your shoulderblades until the arrow hits.
H. Lowering your right elbow at the instant of release.	Make your elbow move backward. It should feel as if it were being *slightly* lifted on the release.
I. Nocking too high.	Find your proper nocking spot (Chapter 5, Step 3) and mark it on the string.
J. Anchoring higher than usual.	Use the *top edge* of your index finger *under* your jawbone as a consistent anchor spot. Check to see that your head is up and in its proper position. Keep your shoulders *down* and back.
K. Leaning toward the target.	Keep your weight evenly divided on both feet and your body erect.
L. Moving your head and chin forward to meet the string.	Keep your head in its proper position and *pull the string to your chin and nose.* Emphasize squeezing of the shoulderblades.
M. A dead release.	Relax the fingers of your string hand and let your hand recoil naturally along your jawbone. Pretend you are "slitting your throat" with your right index finger as it recoils and slides back along your jawbone.

Problem 10: Your Arrows Scatter from Right to Left on the Target Face

Caused By	*Solutions*
A. Any or all reasons for arrows going too far right and too far left.	See Problems 6 and 7.

Caused By	Solutions
B. Allowing your bowsight to weave from side to side on the gold during the aiming step.	Develop sufficient arm and shoulder strength through exercise to hold your sight steady and *precisely* on the proper aiming spot for as long as it needs to be held there (Chapter 10). Practice holding the draw and aiming for as long as you can, gradually increasing the time as your strength increases. (Do *not* release the string. Let it down gently instead.)

Problem 11: Your Arrows Scatter High and Low on the Target Face

Caused By	Solutions
A. Any or all the reasons for arrows going too high and too low.	See Problems 8 and 9.
B. Allowing your bowsight to weave up and down on the gold during aiming.	Develop sufficient arm and shoulder strength through exercise to be able to hold your sight steady and *precisely* where it needs to be (Chapter 10). Practice holding the draw and aim for as long as you can, gradually increasing the time as your strength increases. (Do *not* release. Gently let the string down instead.)

Problem 12: Your Arrows Scatter

Caused By	Solutions
A. Inconsistent shooting form.	Carefully review the nine steps of good target-archery technique (Chapter 5) and

Caused By	*Solutions*

mentally compare them with what you are doing. Having thus discovered your mistakes, begin working to eliminate them, one at a time, beginning with Step 1. Set up a check list for yourself (Chapter 6) and *use it*. *Concentrate* on shooting in good form rather than on shooting for good scores.

B. Inaccurate aiming.

Be sure your sight is *precisely* on the proper aiming spot. *Know* where it is.

Develop strength and endurance in your arm and shoulder muscles to hold steady (Chapter 10).

C. Becoming physically tired and committing many mistakes in shooting technique.

Exercise and running will build muscle strength and endurance (Chapter 10).

D. Mismatched equipment.

Be sure your arrows are matched to your bow and that your bow is "set up" and "tuned-in" (Chapter 9).

E. Crooked arrows.

Get them straightened. If this is impossible, discard them.

Problem 13: Not Holding Long Enough to Get Properly Aimed

Caused By

A. Using a bow which is too heavy for you in your present physical condition.

Solutions

Use a lighter bow. Exercise to develop strength and endurance in your arm, shoulder, and upper back muscles (Chapter 10).

B. Snap shooting.

Practice drawing and holding as long as possible. (Do *not* release. Gently let the string down instead.)

Increase your holding time as your strength increases.

Helen Turnbull, Mesa Community College, Arizona; runner-up, 1969 U. S. Intercollegiate Championships.

tackle "setup" and "tune-in"

Probably one of the most common reasons for arrow scatter on the target face is that equipment is mismatched. To make high scores, it is necessary to have good technique, but even perfect form won't help much if, for instance, your arrows are not matched to your bow draw-weight or if your brace-height varies from session to session. This mismatching is very common with school and camp equipment, but there are many good archers who are shooting with equipment which is not matched. It has been estimated that one out of five skilled archers doesn't know how to adjust his equipment to get the most out of it. When these archers take the time to "set up" their equipment and then "tune it in," their scores will improve.

Have you ever noticed arrows wobbling from side to side or loping up and down on their way to the target? One cause of this is improper bow setup. By this we mean "preparation of your tackle to achieve its top potential." Another cause is failure to tune it in after it is set up. This involves adjusting it so that your arrows fly perfectly.

Let's examine the steps you need to follow to get your tackle set up properly:[1]

1. Be sure that the weight of your bow is realistically within your ability to draw easily and hold steady for at least 10 seconds.

2. A bow with a sight window is preferable to one without, and the closer to the center of the bow limb your arrow lies, the more desirable it is.

3. Attach an arrow rest. Choose one that is semiflexible, either the kind with horizontal feathers or the brush type. These are more forgiving of a slight mistake in your release. Later you may wish to change to a stiffer type, such as metal or plastic. In either case, install your arrow rest ½ inch to ¾ inch above the shelf on your bow so that it is directly above the pivot point on the grip. The width of the arrow rest should never be greater than the diameter of your arrow.

4. It is an advantage to have an arrow plate which is adjustable. This makes it easier to find just the right build-out from center shot for perfect arrow flight. Not all bows are equipped with adjustable plates, but if yours is not, there is a way to build it out from the side of the bow. This will be explained later in the chapter.

5. If you have a detachable stabilizer, and wish to use it, attach it to your bow. Stabilizers affect arrow flight and their use may call for a slightly stiffer arrow. Not all bows come with detachable stabilizers, but instead the manufacturer has extended the handle-riser section beyond the back of the bow

---

1. Many of the ideas included in this chapter have been derived from the 1968 brochure of the Easton Aluminum Arrow Company.

at certain points, and it is claimed that these extensions act as stabilizers. Other bows have no stabilizers of any kind.

6. Attach your bowsight to your bow. Whether it will go on the back or face of the bow is often determined by the shape of the handle-riser section. Many champions mount it on the back and placement there gives you a finer sighting picture because the bowsight is a little farther from your eyes. However, there is nothing wrong with mounting it on the face of your bow; many highly skilled archers prefer it there because it is easier to adjust when changing from one distance to another.

7. Brace your bow. Measure its brace-height with a ruler or a bow square. Check a catalogue or the instructions which came with your bow to find out what brace-height is recommended by the manufacturer, and where it is to be measured. Unless it is specifically stated otherwise, measure the brace-height from the pivot point on the grip to the string. If the height varies from the recommendation, adjust the length of your string until it is correct. This will involve twisting it a little more to shorten it or untwisting it to lengthen it. A string should never have more than 12 full twists in it, so if you need more than that, buy a shorter string. Bow manufacturers have carried out numerous experiments to determine the brace-height that gives the greatest efficiency with each of their models. Go along with their recommendations until you can prove to yourself that a higher brace-height will give you tighter groups and slightly greater cast (but if you get it too high, you will lose cast) or that a lower height will give you a smoother-shooting bow and less string vibration. After you have the string to the proper brace-height, measure it and write the height on a small piece of masking tape attached to the face of the bow on the lower limb, just below the grip. Always measure the brace-height before you shoot

your first arrow. Several times during a shooting session, make sure that it is the height that you have found most efficient.

8. Determine the actual draw-weight of your bow. To do this you must first find out your *actual draw-length.* This is measured from the back of your bow to the bottom of the groove in the arrow nock when you are at full-draw and firmly anchored. There are numerous ways of doing this, the most accurate of which is (1) draw a long arrow several times, in a very lightweight bow; (2) hold your draw; (3) have someone mark the spot on the shaft that is even with the back of your bow; and (4) measure from this mark to the bottom of the groove in the nock. This is your *actual draw-length,* or to put it another way, this is the length arrow you need.

Let's assume, as an example, that the bow weight marked on your bow is 30# (30 pounds), but that no draw-length is indicated. Most bows now (and all bows manufactured under AMO standards in the future) are measured for weight at 28 inches unless a different length is marked on the bow. So you would assume that your bow is 30# at 28 inches. Let's further assume that your actual draw-length is 26 inches. Therefore, when you draw the string back only 26 inches on your bow, it will not require 30 pounds of energy, but something less than that. What is the actual number of pounds of energy needed to pull the string back 26 inches—in other words, what is your actual draw-weight? The old rule for draws other than 28 inches was to subtract two pounds for every inch less and to add two pounds for every inch more. This did not give a very accurate draw-weight, however, so the AMO has devised a uniform rule for bows to be manufactured according to their standards. Their system should give a much more accurate actual draw-weight. Arrows can thus be matched more closely to the bow and will fly more perfectly. The AMO procedure is as follows:

a) Divide the draw-weight marked on the bow by 20.
b) Determine how many inches less (or more) than 28 inches your actual draw is.
c) Multiply the answers from (a) and (b) above.
d) Subtract (or add) the answer obtained in (c) from the weight marked on the bow. This is your *actual draw-weight.*

Using the example cited earlier, you would then divide 30 pounds by 20, giving you 1.50 pounds. Since your draw is two inches less than 28 inches, you would multiply 1.50 pounds by 2, giving you 3 pounds. When you subtract the 3 pounds from the 30 pounds marked on the bow, you would find that you have a 27-pound bow with your 26-inch arrow.

Having thus found your actual draw-weight, write it down on the piece of masking tape where you marked your brace-height. It would be written 27# − 26″.

9. Get arrows that will match the actual draw-weight of your bow so that they will have the correct spine, will clear the bow properly, and will fly perfectly. Buy the best arrows you can afford—aluminum if at all possible.

Archery dealers have charts supplied to them by arrow manufacturers which will tell you exactly what size 26-inch aluminum arrow you need to match your 27-pound bow. (There are similar charts for fiberglass arrows and the AMO has set up some for wooden arrows made according to their standards.) A quick glance would tell you that you need 26-inch aluminum arrows size 1616. The first two digits indicate the diameter of the arrow in 64ths of an inch (16/64″). The last two digits indicate the thickness of the walls of the aluminum tubing in thousandths of an inch (16/1000″). These two factors, diameter and wall thickness, plus the length of your arrow, determine its spine. Therefore, the 26-inch 1616 arrows you have chosen will have just the right amount of spine to bend around the bow as they should; when you release one, it should fly perfectly after it clears the bow (see Chapter 7).

The fletching is important to the flight of an arrow. Its purpose is to stabilize the arrow in flight and this is accomplished by the air resistance to the fletching as the arrow moves toward the target. Your arrow needs to have just enough feather (or vane) surface to stabilize the weight of your arrow. Any excess surface adds weight and more air resistance, and both these factors act as a needless drag on your arrow and slow it down.

Three-fletched arrows should not need feathers longer than 3½ inches or higher than ½ inch. Four-fletched arrows can have smaller feathers because the surface needed to stabilize the same size arrow is still the same, but you have now spread it out on four surfaces instead of three. Fletching should not be heavily spiraled around the shaft; a slight spiral or even parallel fletching is better.

The nock is a vitally important part of your arrow setup. Check to see that it has been put on perfectly straight. Arrows with off-center nocks will fly erratically and will not group properly.

Finally, it is imperative that your shafts be straight. Either take them to a dealer to be straightened or use one of the numerous shaft-straighteners that are on the market.

10. Check your finger protection. If you are using a glove, be sure that it is soft and that it fits properly. The most common mistake made by people who use finger tabs is that they do not trim them down to a size that will give their fingers the needed protection but which eliminates all the excess leather that will deflect the string at the moment of release.

Now your tackle is properly set up to achieve its potential and you are ready to tune it in, or adjust it, to get perfect arrow flight.

1. Determine where your nock-locator should be attached to the serving. If it is not in the correct place, your arrow will lope up and down on the way to the target, and you will get an up-and-down scatter. Max Hamilton's Bare Shaft Test[2] will quickly tell you where to put the nock-locator. With your string at its proper brace-height, mark a spot on your serving which is 1/8 inch above the spot where your arrow would meet the string at right angles. Stand six feet from the target, nock your arrow above the marked spot on your serving, and shoot it into the target, aiming so that it lands at the height of your eyes. After you have two or three arrows in the target at the proper height, check the results of the test:

a) If the shaft is parallel to the ground, you are nocking at the correct place.
b) If the fletching is closer to the ground than the point, you are nocked too low. Raise your pencil mark and continue shooting until the shafts enter parallel to the ground.
c) If your nocks are farther from the ground than your arrow point, you are nocked too high. Lower your nocking point until the shafts enter the target parallel to the ground.

Now attach a nock-locator at the proper spot. Most archers seem to prefer placing it so that they will nock the arrow below it, but there is nothing wrong with placing it so that

2. Max Hamilton, "Bare Shaft Test", *The Archer's Magazine*, Vol. 13, No. 4, April 1964, page 8.

you will nock above it. Some people prefer two locators placed so that they can nock between them. Many archers use a few extra wrappings of dental floss or thread laid in glue so that it will not slip up or down, while others use the slip-on or shrink-on types of locators. All work very satisfactorily; the important thing is to get them firmly attached in the right place.

Once the locator is attached, it is absolutely essential that your brace-height always be the same. If the string stretches, the location of your nocking point will also change, and the same is true if your string shrinks. It is almost impossible to detect these minute changes with the naked eye. This is why you should check the brace-height before you begin shooting and several times during the session. It is also wise to see if your nock-locator has, without your noticing it, become loose so that it slips up and down the string a little bit.

2. Now you must determine whether your arrow plate has the proper build-out from the side of your bow, or sight window. Again, you can use the Hamilton Test, but first lay one of your arrows on the ground in front of your feet so that it points along the intended line-of-flight for your arrows. This time, after you have shot several arrows into the target at the height of your eyes, note the position of the fletching, right to left, in comparison to your intended line-of-flight as indicated by the arrow you put on the ground in front of your feet.

a)   If the fletching is neither to the right nor to the left of your intended line-of-flight, your arrow plate is properly adjusted.

b)   If the fletching is to the left of the intended line-of-flight, move your arrow plate out from the side of your bow. If the plate is not adjustable, remove the arrow rest and put two or three layers of paper behind it. Continue with the test until your arrows enter straight along the intended line-of-flight.

c) If your fletching is to the right of the intended line-of-flight, move the arrow plate in toward the bow or sight window. On bows without adjustable arrow plates, this may involve sanding off some of the wood at the side of the bow to make the bow more center-shot. With lightweight bows, where short arrows are being used, you may find this happening rather frequently. Try moving your arrow rest forward (toward the back of the bow) and see if this will correct the problem before sanding part of the bow away.

3. This step in the tuning-in of your tackle involves the help of another person. Have your helper stand, pencil in hand, face-to-face with you on the shooting line. Put an arrow on the string, assume full draw, and hold it. Now your partner should place a mark on your string which is at the level of your eyes. Check it several times until you have it adjusted properly. Make the pencil mark black enough or wrap a few turns of thread around it as you did for your nock-locator so that you can see where the spot is at full-draw, when your vision is still focused on the gold of the target. When this has been set, take a full draw and note where, on the upper limb of your bow, the black mark comes to rest. Mark that place with a +, and check it out for accurate placement a few times. Thereafter, and on each succeeding shot, line up the black string mark with the crossed lines on the +. This will assure you that your head is always in the same position and that you have anchored in the same place. It furthermore tells you that the distance between your aiming eye and the bowsight is the same on every shot so that you are aiming more consistently.

If you prefer, you could put a peep-sight in your string where the black pencil mark is. In this case, you would then look through the peep-sight at full-draw, and get it and your bowsight so that they were lined up with the spot at which you were aiming at the target.

Target archers should be aware that eye-level marks and string peep-sights are not allowed in the F.I.T.A. Round. This is a rather commonly used round in many local and state meets and is always included as part of the national championships. It will be the round shot in the Olympics and is exclusively used in the World Championships even now. Therefore, if an archer plans to compete in these kinds of events, he would be wise not to become dependent upon these attachments.

Your tackle is now set up and tuned-in so that your arrows fly perfectly out of your bow. Now step back to 15 yards and shoot, working for tight groups. Then move to 30 yards and have a partner watch your arrows in flight to see if they wobble from left to right or lope up and down. If you have made your preparations carefully, they should be flying out of your bow beautifully.

Check your setup and tune-in frequently. A skilled archer must take nothing for granted as far as his equipment is concerned. He must *know* that it is performing to its top potential and that any scattering of arrows on the target is due to imperfections in his personal shooting form. There is no time or place in the middle of a tournament to set up or tune-in your tackle. When you enter a meet, you must have the confidence that comes with knowing that your equipment is in perfect order and that all you have to do is to shoot perfectly. If you lack this confidence, your first misplaced arrow will bring doubts to your mind—"It couldn't be *me*—it must be my equipment." When there are doubts in your mind, your self-confidence is gone, and you shoot poorly. But if you *know* your equipment is in order, all you need to do is to carefully review your check list (Chapter 6) to find what error you made in shooting form, and, having discovered it, correct it. Then you are back in the groove and in control of the situation again. It's as simple as that!

Second United States Intercollegiate Championships (1965).

some scientific aspects of target archery

This chapter deals with some mechanical principles involved in archery and the major muscles used during shooting. Exercises are also included for strengthening the major muscles.

MECHANICAL ASPECTS OF ARCHERY

Motor skills can be analyzed very extensively in relation to the mechanical principles used. Archery will be analyzed very briefly in this chapter in an effort to supply mechanical reasons, or "whys," for basic techniques described throughout the text.

A. Body Position: The first essential for success in archery is the maintenance of an erect, well-balanced standing position. This position is duplicated for every shot at the same distance. Balance can be increased by widening the base of support. This can be accomplished by spreading the feet slightly farther apart. Stability, or balance, is greatest when the center of gravity lies in the center of the base of support; therefore the archer should resist any temptation to lean. The center of gravity is the imaginary "balance center" of the body.

B. The Draw: Although the draw is accomplished primarily by the draw arm, the bow arm must maintain sufficient resistance to overcome the force of the draw. At the full extent of the draw, the bow arm must be firmly "locked" in place. This will enable the bow arm to absorb the force, or reaction, of the bow as the arrow leaves the string. Otherwise the left elbow will bend or slip out of position.

C. Aiming: The flight of the arrow is the same as for all projectiles, meaning that it travels in an arc. Gravitational pull begins to operate immediately on all projectiles. Even at shorter distances the arrow travels in a slight arc, and this arc becomes more apparent as the archer moves farther from the target. When shooting for the greatest distance, an angle of 45° above the horizontal is selected. With equal application of force, this angle-of-flight will result in the greatest distance for the arrow or any other projectile.

D. Release: A smooth release is necessary to impart the full force of the string to the arrow in the direction desired and to prevent unnecessary vibration of the string, which would cause the arrow to weave. Any slight error at the instant of release is magnified during the flight to the target. The greater the distance, the greater the resulting error. At fifty yards from the target, a "creeping" error of less than one inch at release could result in the arrow landing more than a foot from the center of the target.

It is essential that the bow arm, trunk, and legs be firmly locked in place before and during the release to absorb the reaction of the bow. The heavier or more forceful the bow, the more reaction must be absorbed by the archer. Not only is additional strength required to pull a heavier bow, but sufficient body weight is necessary to absorb the more forceful reaction of the heavier bow.

Throughout the discussion of the techniques, there is much emphasis on reproducing *as exactly as possible* the same body position, draw, anchor, aim, release, and follow-through. Mechanically, this is essential if the arrow is to be released at the target from the same position, at the same angle, with the same force, resulting in a repeat of the previous successful attempts.

KINESIOLOGICAL ASPECTS OF ARCHERY

A complete kinesiological or anatomical analysis is far beyond the scope of this text. Reference will be made here only to the *major muscles* of the upper body which are involved in archery. Many of the small muscles of the forearm are not listed in this analysis, although they are important in holding the bow. Strengthening exercises are included for the muscle groups mentioned.

A. Muscular Analysis. When the archer raises the bow and holds it in place, the *deltoid* muscle contracts (Fig. 10-1a). The middle part of the deltoid is primarily responsible for holding the weight of the bow. The back part of the deltoid contracts vigorously on the draw arm as the draw occurs and it also works on the bow arm to help stabilize that arm. The *pronator teres* is responsible for keeping the bow arm elbow rotated out so that the string will not chafe the inner arm (Fig. 10-1b).

The *triceps,* which is the large muscle on the back of the upper arm, is primarily responsible for keeping the bow arm extended, or locked in place (Fig. 10-1a). The *biceps,* located on the front of the upper arm, contracts to bend the draw arm

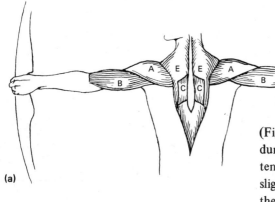

(a)

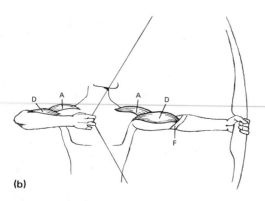

(b)

Fig. 10-1 (a) Back view of upper-body muscles: A, deltoids; B, triceps; C, rhomboids; E, trapezius. (b) Front view of upper-body muscles: A, deltoids; D, biceps; F, pronator teres.

(Fig. 10-1b). The biceps of the bow arm is generally relaxed during the draw to avoid excess tension in the arm. Excessive tension is exceedingly damaging to skilled activity because a slight shaking occurs as one muscle temporarily overpowers the other.

Perhaps the most important muscles in archery are small thin bands stretching from the *scapula*, or shoulderblade, to the spine. These are the *rhomboids* and they are responsible for drawing the shoulders back to what is normally referred to as "good posture" (Fig. 10-1a). The rhomboids are in constant contraction during the entire process of draw-aim-release-follow-through, and they are responsible for the elastic-like sensation the archer feels if he alternately draws and relaxes the string. The *trapezius* muscle lies over the rhomboids and the middle portion aids in drawing the shoulderblades together (Fig. 10-1a). The lower portion of the *trapezius* keeps the shoulders from hunching up.

B. Arm and Shoulder Exercises. Most activities do not make sufficient demands on the muscles involved to increase strength. To draw his bow with comparative ease and hold it steady, the archer needs to strengthen the muscles involved. Many skilled performers therefore engage in supplementary exercises which *overload* the muscles involved in the activity. The overload principle refers to subjecting a muscle to loads greater than it is normally accustomed. One method of doing this is to repeatedly draw a bow that is heavier than the one used in shooting. Another method is to perform a series of exercises designed to make use of the muscles involved in archery.

Triceps Exercises

1. Push-ups (without apparatus):

a) Body straight, arms straight, weight on hands and toes.

b) Bend arms, keeping the body straight.

c) Bring the chin to within an inch of the floor;

d) Push up and return to the starting position. (Girls may perform the push-ups with the weight on the hands and knees)

2. Overhead or military press (with weights):

a) Bring bar to rest and support at the shoulders.

b) Press directly above the head until arms are straight.

c) Return bar to the rest position.

3. Dips (on the parallel bars):

a) Move to an arm-support position with the body and arms straight.

b) Dip or bend the elbows until the hands are even with the chest.

c) Push back up to the arm-support position.

Biceps Exercises

1. Chins (horizontal bar):

a) Grasp the bar, palms toward the face, and hang with the arms straight.

b) Pull up until the chin clears the bar.

c) Return to hanging position.

2. Isometric curl (with a partner):

a) Bend arms at the elbow, at 90°, palms up.

b) Partner holds wrists and resists continued bending.

c) Hold for ten seconds and then relax.

3. Curl (with weights):

a) Bring the bar to rest at the thighs, with the palms out.

b) "Curl" the bar, or bend the arm until the bar touches the chest below the chin.

c) Return slowly to the starting position.

Forearm Exercises

1. Wrist roller (with weights):

a) Weight is attached to a short bar or stick by four or five feet of rope.

b) Hold bar out at arms length at shoulder height, with the weight rolled down.

c) Roll the weight up on the bar by alternately turning the wrists clockwise.

d) Roll the weights downward by counterclockwise rotation of the wrists.

2. Isometric pronation (with partner):

a) Shake hands with partner, using the bow hand.

b) Attempt to turn the palm down as your partner resists.

c) Hold for 10 seconds, then relax.

3. Wrist curl (with weight):

a) Sit on a bench with the elbows and forearm resting on the thighs, and the bar in your hands.

b) Allow the bar to roll down to your finger tips and then curl it back up with the wrists, keeping the forearm in contact with the thigh.

c) Relax and allow the bar to roll down the fingers again.

Deltoid Exercises

1. Isometric lateral raise (with a partner):

a) Raise straightened arm to the side.

b) Partner grasps wrist and resists movement above the horizontal.

c) Hold for ten seconds and then relax.

2. Lateral raises (with weight):

a) Hold weights at side, arms straight.

b) Raise arms to the side, keeping them straight.

c) After reaching the horizontal position, stop and return arms to the sides.

Rhomboid and Trapezius Exercises

1. Isometric chest stretcher (with partner):

a) Hold arms up at chest, bent at the elbow.

b) Partner stands behind the exerciser and holds elbows, resisting the backward movement of the arms.

c) Hold resistance for 10 seconds and then relax.

2. Chest stretcher (with weight):

a) Hold arms with weights in hands, at chest level and straight ahead.

b) Pull arms back, bending the elbows until the shoulder-blades touch.

c) Return to the original position.

The exercises suggested above involve either movement or maintaining a motionless state against resistance. The resistance, which comes from weight apparatus, body weight, or a partner, is the overload needed to develop strength. Most calesthenics do not offer resistance, and thus will not develop strength. Many exercise gadgets will offer sufficient resistance to overload the muscles either through moving (isotonic) exercises or static (isometric) exercises.

It is strongly suggested that the muscle-strengthening program be started *before* the archery season begins. Once it has gotten under way, strengthening exercises should be carried out *after* the archer has completed shooting for the day; otherwise fatigue may interfere with shooting accuracy.

Bob Burcaw, Michigan State University, and Hardy Ward, Kilgore (Texas) College, 1969 United States Intercollegiate Champion.

suggestions for teaching and coaching target archery

This chapter is designed to present a few ideas which have proved helpful in working with individuals or groups of archers to make them more skillful. It is not intended to be a plan of what you are to teach day by day because no two people are alike, and no two would go about teaching archery in precisely the same manner.

For purposes of clarification, when you are working with two or more individuals, you are teaching; when you work with one individual, you are coaching. Some of the suggestions which follow apply best to a teaching situation, while others are more applicable during coaching sessions. At the end of each of the nine steps in the technique of target archery, as presented in Chapter 5, you will find additional coaching hints.

Suggested class progressions for archers of varying degrees of skill are listed at the end of the chapter. Instructors in camps and schools will find these particularly helpful because they can be adapted to whatever length of time is available.

Both the Professional Archers Association and the American Indoor Archery Association have well-developed plans for teaching archery, and any P.A.A. member or indoor archery-lanes operator can give you information concerning them. Detailed lesson plans have been purposely left out since you must take into consideration so many local circumstances as you plan a lesson for a class.

1. Keep in mind that you are teaching and coaching a *person,* and that archery is the vehicle you are using to help him become a better person.

2. Keep your voice calm, interesting, enthusiastic, and loud enough to be heard by your group. Your voice is your most important teaching tool. Make good use of it.

3. Stand where you can see all your students and they can see you. Eye contact with all of your students is vital to good teaching.

4. Give each member of a class the feeling that you are truly interested in him as a person and as an archer.

5. Keep your class informal, relaxed, and fun, but always under control and safe.

6. Children are impatient, and the younger they are the more impatient they are. So talk less and have them *do* more.

7. Progress and improvement should be made in each lesson for each student.

8. Allow time for questions. This may point out to you where you need to review or where you did a poor job of teaching.

9. Archers can't work on everything at once, so work on what is most important *at that stage.*

10. You need your hands when you are teaching. Sometimes you almost have to do the motions for the students. At

other times, a little pressure here or a finger touching there will help them develop a kinesthetic awareness.

11. Talk as little as possible, but *say what you mean* and mean what you say.

12. Use words your archers understand, words that are at *their* level of understanding. You may have to coin words or phrases to get your ideas across to them.

13. Prevent bad habits from forming. It's easier to learn a skill the right way in the beginning than to have to break a bad habit and relearn the skill the correct way. It takes 8 or 10 good shots to counteract one bad shot.

14. Be patient. You may have to repeat some explanations or demonstrations many times. Not everybody will understand your first explanation, although they will *tell* you they do, and they will *look* as if they do. Devise other ways of saying the same thing.

15. Check the school or camp policy concerned with allowing archers to shoot outside of class time. If there is no policy, establish one in conference with the proper camp or school authorities. The safest policy is that no one may use the range or equipment unless an instructor is present.

16. Remember there is no "one best way" to teach or coach archery. Keep an open mind. Read and seek out help on things you don't know or don't understand. If things come up in class that you don't know, admit it, but find out before the next lesson and inform the group of your findings. Every time you work with students in archery, you will probably learn more than the students. There is no end to learning about archery.

17. Compliment good form. Compliment good scores. In fact, when a student does something well, let him know that *you* recognize his skill or knowledge. Nothing is as successful as success.

18. Be efficient and don't waste valuable time. While waiting for slow-shooting archers to finish, work behind the shooting line with those who have special problems.

19. Relate archery to things which the students already know or with which they have already had experience. For instance, with many boys and some girls you can explain that the anchor point is like the rear sight on a rifle and the bowsight is like the front sight. Aiming with both front and rear sights makes for greater accuracy than aiming with just one.

20. Watch the positions the archer gets into and be ready with quick suggestions to correct them.

21. When you are coaching an individual, watch *him* rather than the arrow or target.

22. Do not allow archers to shoot without wearing both an armguard and a finger tab or glove. *Prevent* sore fingers and bruised arms. Some people have very tender fingers and they may get sore even with protection. Skin can be toughened by painting it with tincture of benzoin, which is available at all drugstores. The liquid should be painted on several times before the shooting season begins and then occasionally during the year, as the need arises.

23. Assign students to lightweight bows at first, so that they can draw the string back to their noses easily and without strain. They will thus develop *good* shooting habits, will have better scores, and will enjoy archery more.

24. Assign beginners to arrows that are at least two inches too long for them. This will minimize the danger of overdrawing the arrow and injuring themselves when they release.

25. Don't let your students *release* a string without an arrow on it. They may, however, when they are learning the draw and anchor, draw the string back to the tip of their

noses, but they should then let it down to brace-height slowly and easily.

26. Get students shooting as soon as is possible, but not so soon that safety is neglected.

27. Don't try to give students every detail in the first lesson. Decide what is most important and what must be covered first and then emphasize that. Many details can be added later. For example, in their first lesson tell them that the bowsight aims the point of the arrow, but don't dwell on it in detail *at this time*. Use one in your demonstration and tell them you will explain its use later. As another example, they should be *very clear* on what is the proper position of the left elbow, and should practice getting it rotated into its position. No archer should injure his arm and elbow by having it slapped by the string on release. This one injury has caused more people to dislike archery than any other, and it is an injury they never seem to forget.

28. Don't be too analytical and don't expect too much at first. The first experience in shooting should be an enjoyable one.

29. For the first few lessons, if you brace the bows up beforehand, it will save time and get your students shooting sooner. Teach bracing techniques about the fourth lesson. Recent experiments have shown that fiberglass and composite bows can be left braced for a period of several months without damage to the bow. If you have these bows, you may want to leave them braced for the camp session, or until the end of the archery unit in school. You could thus eliminate from your program the technique of bracing and unbracing a bow. (Of course, this could be a disadvantage if a student had to find someone to brace his bow for him every time he wanted to shoot.)

30. This is not a rhythmical sport. Let students release when they feel they are ready. Don't have them release on a count or command from you.

31. Don't have students hold at full-draw for very long at the beginning. They usually don't have the muscular strength to do so. Let them release when they are in a reasonably good position and correct them before the next shot.

32. Ask students questions to get them to analyze their own form. This also gives you some clues concerning how well they know what they are trying to make themselves do.

33. The aiming process needs to be explained several times. This is the one step in which the coach cannot detect errors. You can't *see* what the archer is seeing, so you never know if he has the right picture during the aiming step. He must understand thoroughly what he should be seeing and doing.

34. Have your equipment properly marked and identified, particularly bows and arrows. Devise a system and explain it to your students, so that they always get the same bow, and arrows of the length assigned to them. *They should know they have the right equipment.*

35. Store equipment properly and insist that your students return it properly to its place. Give them ample time to get this job done.

36. Instruct your students in the proper care of archery equipment and insist that they follow your instructions.

37. Keep archery tackle in good repair and check it frequently. Teach your students to check the equipment they are using before they shoot with it.

38. Archers should have enough room on the shooting line so that it is possible for them to practice good shooting technique without danger to themselves or to the archers near them.

39. Use exercises which will strengthen the upper arm and upper back muscles. In a shooting lesson, do the exercises at the end of the period; in a nonshooting lesson do them at the beginning of the lesson. It is wise to begin the archery exercises before the lessons have begun—perhaps a week ahead of time—to build the required strength to efficiently handle the bow and arrow. Encourage archers to include these exercises as part of their daily fitness program.

40. There is less chance of an injury to a passerby if arrows that miss the target are landing low, rather than high. Place the target faces as low on the butts as is possible, especially with beginners.

41. Teach, practice, and enforce safety precautions at all times. Make your students and yourself safety conscious. *Every* aspect of the archery program must be safe. A bow and arrow is a dangerous weapon. It is certainly not a plaything.

42. Wait until your students stop talking before you begin to explain anything. Get their attention before you begin.

Fig. 11-1 Suggested progressions for target archery classes.

	Beginners' Level	Intermediate Level	Advanced Level
Part 1	10 yards	20 yards	30 yards
	48-inch face	24-inch face	16-inch face
	3 hours	3 hours	3 hours
	Safety rules; Care of equipment	Review bracing and unbracing	Hamilton Test
		History of archery	Current uses of archery
Part 2	15 yards	30 yards	40 yards
	48-inch face	24-inch face	24-inch face
	3 hours	3 hours	3 hours
	Scoring	Hamilton Test	Assigned readings in archery
	Bracing and unbracing		

Fig. 11-1 (cont.)

	Beginners' Level	Intermediate Level	Advanced Level
Part 3	20 yards 48-inch face 3 hours Arrow lecture	40 yards 24-inch face 3 hours Double scoring and tournament procedure	50 yards 80-cm face 3 hours
Part 4	25 yards 48-inch face 3 hours Bow lecture	50 yards 48-inch face 3 hours	60 yards 48-inch face 3 hours
Part 5	30 yards 48-inch face 3 hours Double scoring	Replacing nocks Starting and ending a serving Fletching demonstration Teach string-making 3 hours	Tournament: Columbia Round Review string-making, fletching, nock replacement Teach arrow-straightening 3 hours
Part 6	Tournament 24 arrows at 30, 25, 20 yards, 48-inch face 3 hours	Tournament: Columbia Round 3 hours	Junior American Round: Class Tournament 3 hours
Part 7	35 yards 48-inch face 3 hours	Scholastic Round Tournament: 24 arrows at 40, 30; 48-inch face 3 hours	American Round Tournament 3 hours
Part 8	30 yards 24-inch face 3 hours	50 yards, 48-inch face; 1 hour Columbia Round 2 hours	Enter interschool, etc. tournaments as available 3 hours
Part 9	Class tournament: 24 arrows, 35, 30 yards, 24-inch face 3 hours or Novelty event	Class tournament: Columbia Round 3 hours or Novelty event	Enter tournaments as available 3 hours or Novelty event

In addition, students at all three levels should learn or review the following:

1. Bracing and unbracing a bow
2. Parts of the bow and arrow
3. Care of equipment
4. Safety
5. Rules and scoring
6. Terminology
7. Shooting technique—nine steps.

As can readily be seen, many of the things suggested for inclusion in the classes might be impossible to do because of your particular situation. As an example, if all your students are shooting 20-pound bows, it would be fruitless to have them shoot from 40 or 50 yards, because most bows that light will not carry an arrow accurately for that distance. You would need to make adjustments in the plan to fit your needs. You might want to keep them at 30 yards but use a smaller face than that recommended.

It should also be noted that the total time allotted for the progressions is 27 hours of class time. You may not have that much time available and would have to choose what to eliminate. It is recommended that you trim off as many of the last parts of the plan as is necessary, rather than cut Parts 1, 2, or 3.

If you lack the distances suggested, you can make adjustments in the progressions by shortening the distances and using smaller target faces.

Pete Arballo, City College of San Jose at the United States Intercollegiate Championships in 1969.

rules for target archery; rounds; scoring

The National Archery Association of the United States is the recognized governing body for archery. It represents the United States on the U.S. Olympic Committee and in the International Archery Federation and is therefore in charge of setting up qualifications for and the method to be used in selecting any team that is to represent the United States of America in competition. This includes teams for The Ambassador's Cup matches with Canada, the World Field Archery Championships, the World Target Archery Championships and, beginning in 1972, the Olympic archery teams.

The N.A.A. rules which follow are those in effect for official target archery tournaments.[1] There are additional and somewhat different rules in effect when archers shoot the F.I.T.A. Round. Complete rule books containing N.A.A.,

---

1. October 1968, revised edition.

F.I.T.A., and some of the Olympic rules are available from the Executive Secretary of the N.A.A.[2]

N.A.A. OFFICIAL TOURNAMENT RULES

The rules contained herein govern conduct and competition in the National Archery Association Annual Tournament and all six-golds tournaments that are officially recognized by the National Archery Association.

Because local conditions may prevent elaborate field arrangements, properties, or personnel usage, *minimum rules* are stated and allowable tolerances are indicated. In the interests of uniformity, local clubs and associations are urged to adopt these rules to govern local archery competition.

Such local clubs or associations may adopt special regulations or additional rules, providing that such additions do not conflict with, or in any way alter, one or more rules contained herein.

Decisions not regulated by the Official Tournament Rules of the National Archery Association, or by specific regulations of local clubs and associations, shall fall under the authority of the tournament officials involved.

PRIMARY RULES

Safety and Courtesy

A. Every precaution must be taken to ensure the highest possible safety standards. This has precedence over all other consideration or rules. Any practices, attitudes, equipment, or conditions, either mentioned herein, or not mentioned herein, which are in the least degree unsafe, are prohibited. Repeti-

---

2. Mr. Clayton Shenk, 2833 Lincoln Highway East, Ronks, Pa., 17572.

tion, after one warning by a tournament official, shall require the offending participant, or participants, to be expelled from the tournament without refund. It shall be the responsibility of every N.A.A. member to insist upon strict maintenance of safety standards at all times.

B.   To ensure a fair enjoyment of archery competition by all contestants, a high standard of personal courtesy and sportsmanship is enjoined upon all. Discourteous or unsportsmanlike conduct is an unwarranted offense against other archers and an affront to the heritage of dignity and tradition which is an integral part of the sport of archery. Persistance in discourteous or unsportsmanlike conduct shall, after one warning from the tournament official, be considered grounds for expulsion from the tournament, without refund, of the offending participants.

1.0 The Archery Range

1.1   The target field shall be laid out so that shooting is from South to North. A maximum deviation of 45° is allowed for the N.A.A. Annual Tournaments. Local tournament deviation from this rule is allowed, if required by terrain available.

1.2   The targets shall be equally spaced five, plus or minus one, yards (four to six yards) apart, measured from the center of the gold to the center of the gold of the adjacent target.

1.3   Range distances shall be accurately measured from a point on the ground perpendicular to the center of the gold on the target face to the shooting point.

1.4   Target lines and shooting lines, or range lines, shall be plainly and accurately marked on the ground, and shall be not more than six inches in width. Target lines or shooting lines may be arranged to require the shooters to move forward from the longest range to the lesser distances while the targets remain stationary, or to require the targets to be brought forward from longer to lesser distances while the shooters use a stationary line.

1.5 Individual target lanes shall be suitably and plainly marked either by a center line, or by lines designating the side boundaries of each lane. Pegs, chalk lines, trenches, or mowed strips are suitable markings. Local tournaments may deviate from this rule.

1.6 There shall be a minimum of 20 yards clear space behind the targets, which may be reduced by a suitable bunker or backstop. Spectators, participants, or pedestrians shall not be allowed behind the targets while shooting is in progress, or even beyond 20 yards if there is the slightest possibility of being struck by the wildest arrow.

1.7 There shall be a clear area of at least 20 yards on each side of the field as a safety lane.

1.8 Bow racks, tackle boxes, or other objects which protrude above the ground shall not be allowed within six feet of the shooting line.

1.9 At least every third target should have a small wind flag, of a size and color easily visible from the 100-yard line, mounted at least two feet above the top of the target. Local tournaments may deviate from this rule.

1.10 Staggered shooting lines, wherein one group of archers shoot from a position forward of another group, are considered unsafe. In an emergency they may be used provided an unused lateral safety lane of at least 20 yards is maintained as a buffer.

2.0 Target Butts

2.1 The target backstop shall be of any suitable material that will not damage arrows nor allow them to pass through or bounce out frequently.

2.2 The target backstop shall be not less than 50 inches in diameter.

2.3   Target backstops shall be securely anchored to the ground to prevent accidental toppling.

2.4   Target identification shall be by means of numerals at least 8 inches high, on soft cardboard or other suitable material, so as to be easily visible at 100 yards, and should be mounted near the base of the target.

3.0 The Target Face

3.1   The Official Target Face of the N.A.A. must be used for the N.A.A. Annual Tournament and all official six-golds shoots.

3.2   The target face may be of any suitable material that will not damage arrows and that will retain stability of size, shape, and color under adverse weather conditions.

3.3   The scoring area of the target face shall be forty-eight (48) inches in diameter. The target face is divided into five concentric color-zones arranged from the center outwards as follows: gold (yellow), red, blue, black, and white. Each color zone is in turn divided by a thin line, not more than 1/10 inch in width, into two zones of equal width, thus making in all, 10 scoring zones of equal width measured from the center of the gold. Such dividing lines which may be used between colors shall be entirely within the higher-scoring zone.

3.4   Target face colors should be reasonably "dull" and "non-glaring" and conform as closely as possible to the following color code, as specified in the Munsell Color Charts. Colors are listed from the center out.

Color	Hue	Value	Chroma	Notation
gold (yellow)	6.5Y	8.1	10.7	5.0Y -8.0-12.0
red	8.5R	4.9	12.6	5.0R -4.0-14.0
blue	5.0B	6.5	8.0	5.0B -7.0 6.0
black	1.5RP	2.9	0.3	None 2.0-0.0
white	0.5GY	8.94	0.6	None-9.0-0.0

3.5 The center of the gold on the target face shall be mounted 51 inches from the ground. Schools and camps may omit this requirement. The target face shall be inclined away from the shooting line at an angle of from 12 to 18 degrees from the vertical.

4.0 Definitions

4.1 *Shooting area.* An area starting at the shooting line and extending six feet to the rear, and which runs parallel to and adjacent to the shooting line.

4.2 *Tackle and bench area.* An area starting at the rear limit of the Shooting Area and extending six feet to the rear, and which runs parallel to and adjacent to the shooting area.

4.3 *Spectators' area.* The area behind the Tackle and Bench Area.

4.4 *Completed end.* A field official shall signal the finish of each end. Unless this signal is immediately challenged by those archers who have not released six arrows, the end shall be considered complete and the archer shall have no recourse to shooting additional arrows.

4.6 *Perfect end.* Six consecutive arrows in the gold in one end shall constitute a perfect end.

5.0 Archery Tackle

5.1 Any kind of bow may be used, providing it is shot by holding it in one hand and the string in the other, without mechanical assistance or support which in the opinion of the tournament officials would give undue advantage over other competitors.

5.2 Any kind of arrow may be used provided that it does not, in the opinion of the tournament officials, damage the targets unreasonably.

5.3 Any type of sight or aiming device attached to the bow may be used. Any type of point-of-aim may be used which does not protrude more than six inches above ground and does not interfere with shooting or scoring.

5.4   Any type of releasing aid, such as gloves, tabs, straps, flippers, ledges, and other developments of traditional release aids, is permitted, except that mechanical releases consisting of two or more working parts are not permitted. Unusual release aids should be submitted to the tournament officials for eligibility before shooting.

5.5   Any type of artificial spotting aid may be used, provided it be restricted for use behind the shooting area. An archer may not interrupt his shooting turn to use a spotting aid.

5.6   Foot markers may be left on the shooting line during the round provided they are embedded in the turf and do not extend more than ½ inch above ground.

5.7   Ground quivers may be placed on the shooting line while the archer is in the process of shooting but must be removed to the tackle area while others are shooting and during the scoring interval.

6.0 Eligibility and Classification

6.1   Archers shall be classed in the following groups:

a) Men   18 years old or over
b) Women   18 years old or over
c) Intermediate Boys   15 to 18 years old
d) Intermediate Girls   15 to 18 years old
e) Junior Boys   12 to 15 years old
f) Junior Girls   12 to 15 years old
g) Cadet Boys[1]   less than 12 years old
h) Cadet Girls[1]   less than 12 years old

6.2   An archer must shoot in the highest class if the start of the tournament shall be on or after the birthday which places

---

1.   May also be called Beginners.

him in the higher class. However, an archer whose birthday occurs after March 31st in the year of his/her 12th, 15th, or 18th birthday shall be permitted to compete in the lower age group until October 1st of the same year.

6.3   An archer may, by election before shooting starts, compete in a higher class than normally classed, but may not shoot in a lower class. This includes the right of women or girls to compete against men or boys in higher classes, but does not permit men or boys to compete against girls' or women's classes.

6.4   No archer shall be barred from a tournament because of a physical handicap unless his or her shooting requires mechanical aids, which, in the judgment of the Field Officials, would give him or her undue advantage over other archers.

7.0 Field Officials

7.1   Field Officials shall be appointed by the tournament officials and shall rank in authority as follows: Field Captain, Lady Paramount, Assistants to the Field Captain, Assistants to Lady Paramount.

7.2   The Field Officials shall have the responsibility and authority to organize, supervise, and regulate all practice, shooting, and competition in accordance with regulations and customs; to interpret and to decide questions of rules; *to maintain safety conditions;* to enforce sportsmanlike behavior; to score doubtful arrows; to signal the start, interruptions, delays, postponements, and finish of competition.

7.3   Repeated rules infractions or discourteous or unsportsmanlike conduct, not sufficiently grave as to require expulsion, shall be penalized by the Field Officials after an appropriate warning, as follows: for the first repetition after warning, the loss of the highest scoring arrow of that end; for the second repetition, the loss of the end; for the third repetition, expulsion from the tournament without refund.

7.4 Decisions of the lesser field officials shall be final unless immediately appealed to the Field Captain.

7.5 Decisions of the Field Captain shall be final unless immediate verbal notice of intent to protest is given the Field Captain and unless this is followed by the submission of a written protest to the Tournament Chairman within three hours of the completion of the tournament. Written protests will be reviewed by the Governing Board as soon as it can conveniently convene.

8.0 Shooting, Scoring, and Conduct of Participants

8.1 Initial target assignments may be made according to any system designated by the tournament officials. There shall be not less than three nor more than five archers assigned to each target in use, and four is customary.

8.2 Archers shall be reassigned targets after each round on the basis of their total score for rounds completed.

8.3 There shall be at least three uninterrupted practice ends, at the longest distance, followed without interruption by the beginning of scoring for the round.

8.4 There shall be no practice permitted after a postponement or delay unless such postponement or delay exceeds thirty (30) minutes. In such cases, the amount of practice shall be according to the following schedule:

a) Thirty (30) to sixty (60) minute delay; one practice end.

b) Sixty (60) minutes or more delay, unless interrupted by a scheduled lunch period or night fall: two practice ends.

8.5 A blast of the whistle shall be the signal to commence or cease shooting for each end. Two or more blasts signal an immediate interruption for all shooting.

8.6   An archer shall stand so that he has one foot on each side of the shooting line. He shall also stand 18 inches away from the center of the target lane or 18 inches from the boundaries.

8.7   If an archer shoots less than 6 arrows in one end, he may shoot the remaining arrows if the omission is discovered before the end is officially completed, otherwise they shall score as misses (See 4.5).

8.8   If an archer shoots more than 6 arrows in an end, only the lowest 6 shall score.

8.9   Archers may not make up lost rounds, ends, or arrows except as specified.

8.10 If a target falls before an end is scored, that end shall be shot over by all the archers on that target.

8.11 Equipment failures, mishaps, or other occurrences not specifically covered in other rules, shall not entitle an archer to repeat a shot unless the mis-shot arrow can be reached by the bow from the archer's position on the shooting line.

8.12 Arrows in the standard target face shall be evaluated as follows; gold 9; red 7; blue 5; black 3; white 1. Each color zone is in turn divided into two zones of equal width, thus making in all ten (10) scoring zones of equal width. The zones are scored from the center outward; 10, 9, 8, 7, 6, 5, 4, 3, 2, 1.

8.13 If an arrow in the target touches two scoring areas, breaking the outside edge of the black scoring line, the higher score shall count. Doubtful arrows must be determined for each end before the arrows or target face have been touched, otherwise the lower value must be taken.

8.14 An arrow that has passed through the scoring face so that it is not visible from the front shall count 7 at 60 yards or less, and 5 for ranges beyond 60 yards. Arrows passing completely through the target, if witnessed, are scored in the same manner.

8.15 An arrow which rebounds from the scoring face, if witnessed, shall score the same as a pass-through.

8.16 An arrow embedded in another arrow on the scoring face shall score the same as the arrow in which it is embedded.

8.17 If an arrow should hang from the scoring face, shooting shall be interrupted and a Field Official shall immediately reinsert the arrow in its proper place on the scoring face.

8.18 Hits on the wrong target shall score as misses.

8.19 The archer chosen to pull the arrows from the target, normally the first in the order of assignment, shall be the Target Captain and shall rule all questions on his target, subject to appeal to the Field Officials.

8.20 The Target Captain shall call the value of each arrow as he pulls it from the target and it shall then be recorded independently by two contestants acting as scorers, normally the next two assigned to the target. Scorers should check results after each end to avoid errors.

8.21 Each archer is individually responsible for seeing that his arrows are called correctly and properly entered on the score cards, and that his score cards are turned in to the proper officials.

8.22 Any archer should call to the attention of the Field Officials any rule infractions, unsportsmanlike or unseemly conduct, or any *safety hazards*. The Field Officials are empowered to take such steps as their judgment indicates to correct the situation, including warning, scoring penalties, and even expulsion from the tournament in severe cases (See 7.2).

8.23 Any archer may retire from the shooting line to avoid proximity to tackle or a shooting practice that he considers unsafe, and may resume shooting when safe conditions prevail.

8.24 Archers may not shoot at varying distances from different shooting lines, nor engage in unauthorized practice, unless separated laterally by the width of at least four target lanes.

8.25 In all official six-golds shoots, ends shall be shot "three and three." Half (or the closest possible number to half) of the archers assigned to each target shall take position and shoot three arrows each. They shall then retire and the remaining archers assigned to that target shall shoot three arrows each. Then the first group shall shoot their remaining three arrows. Finally, the second group on each target shall shoot their remaining three arrows. The Field Captain may require shooting six arrows at a time only in an emergency where the time saved is necessary to complete the schedule.

8.26 Tie scores shall be resolved in favor of the archer shooting the highest score at the longest distance, then the next longest distance, then through the next longest distances in descending order. If still tied through all distances, then ties shall be resolved in favor of the archer with the greatest total number of golds, then reds, then blues, then blacks. If still tied, the tie shall be resolved in favor of the archer having the greatest total number of perfect ends. If still tied, it shall be so recorded.

8.27 Coaching an archer on the shooting line by means of inaudible and inconspicuous signs or symbols is permitted, providing that such coaching is not distracting to other contestants. If a contestant on the same target or any adjacent one complains that such activity is personally distracting, such coaching must be terminated immediately. Audible coaching of archers on the shooting line is not permitted.

9.0 Rounds

9.1 Championship Rounds

a) The Men's F.I.T.A. Round (F.I.T.A. rules apply)
    36 arrows at 90 meters (98.4 yards), 122-cm 10-ring target face.

36 arrows at 70 meters (76.6 yards), 122-cm 10-ring target face.

36 arrows at 50 meters (54.7 yards), 80-cm 10-ring target face.

36 arrows at 30 meters (32.8 yards), 80-cm 10-ring target face.

b) The Ladies F.I.T.A. Round (F.I.T.A. rules apply)

36 arrows at 70 meters (76.6 yards), 122-cm 10-ring target face.

36 arrows at 60 meters (65.6 yards), 122-cm 10-ring target face.

36 arrows at 50 meters (54.7 yards), 80-cm 10-ring target face.

36 arrows at 30 meters (32.8 yards), 80-cm 10-ring target face.

c) 900 Round (Men, Women, Intermediate Boys and Girls; standard 48 in. target face; scored 10, 9, 8, 7, 6, 5, 4, 3, 2, 1)

30 arrows at 60 yards; 30 arrows at 50 yards; 30 arrows at 40 yards.

d) American Round (Men, Women, Intermediate Boys and Girls; standard 48-inch target face)

30 arrows at 60 yards; 30 arrows at 50 yards; 30 arrows at 40 yards.

9.2 Nonchampionship Rounds

a) Junior American Round (Junior Boys and Girls; standard 48-inch target face)

30 arrows at 50 yards; 30 arrows at 40 yards; 30 arrows at 30 yards.

b) Junior Columbia Round (all Beginners—those under 12 years of age; standard 48-inch target face)

24 arrows at 40 yards; 24 arrows at 30 yards; 24 arrows at 20 yards.

c) York Round (Men; standard 48-inch target face)
72 arrows at 100 yards; 48 arrows at 80 yards; 24 arrows at 60 yards.

d) National Round (Women and Intermediate Girls; standard 48-inch face)
48 arrows at 60 yards; 24 arrows at 50 yards.

e) Columbia Round (Women; Intermediate Girls; Junior Girls; standard 48-inch target face)
24 arrows at 50 yards; 24 arrows at 40 yards; 24 arrows at 30 yards.

f) Hereford Round (Women and Intermediate Boys; standard 48-inch target face)
72 arrows at 80 yards; 48 arrows at 60 yards; 24 arrows at 50 yards.

g) Duryea Round (Men and Women; standard 48-inch target face)[1]
90 arrows at 30 yards.

h) Chicago Round (Men and Women; 16-inch 5-colored target face)
96 arrows at 20 yards.

i) 300 indoor round (16-inch black-and-white target face divided into 5 zones of equal width and scored from the center outward 5, 4, 3, 2, 1)
60 arrows at 20 yards.

j) Junior Boys Hereford Round (standard 48-inch target face)
72 arrows at 50 yards; 48 arrows at 40 yards; 24 arrows at 30 yards.

k) Cadet Girls National Round (Standard 48-inch target face)
48 arrows at 30 yards; 24 arrows at 20 yards.

---

1. The N.A.A. is considering changing this to a 24-inch face.

l) Cadet Girls Columbia Round (standard 48-inch target face)
24 arrows at 40 yards; 24 arrows at 20 yards.

m) Junior Girls National Round (standard 48-inch target face)
48 arrows at 40 yards; 24 arrows at 30 yards.

n) Cadet Boys Hereford Round (Standard 48-inch target face)
36 arrows at 40 yards; 24 arrows at 30 yards; 12 arrows at 20 yards.

o) Cadet American Round (Boys and Girls; standard 48-inch target face)
15 arrows at 30 yards; 15 arrows at 20 yards.

RECORDING SCORES

Before proceeding further with this topic, it might be wise for you to reread Rule 8 concerning scores and scoring.

The so-called "Double Scoring System," involving the use of two scorers per target to avoid mistakes in recording and adding, is described in Rules 8.19 and 8.20. It is highly recommended that the Double Scoring System be used for all tournaments, whether they are run by mail, telegraph, or as actual shoulder-to-shoulder meets where your competition is standing on the shooting line with you. Archers *do* have difficulties with recording and adding scores, and under the pressures of tournament competition this weakness is even more apparent. Tournament officials, teachers, coaches, and camp counselors will save themselves hours of tedious checking of scoresheets when the meet is over if they simply insist on the use of the Double Scoring System.

Keep in mind that the rules pertaining to scoring apply to tournament competition and need not be followed completely during class instruction or practice sessions. At times such as these, you might prefer to have each archer keep his own score so that all learn to do it properly. This will hasten the process of scoring and allow more shooting time.

A scoresheet or scorecard to be used in target archery is shown in Fig. 12-1.

On the score sheet the "H" stands for "hits in the scoring area of the target face," and includes witnessed rebounds and pass-throughs in the scoring area. The "S" stands for "total score for the arrows which hit the scoring area, including witnessed rebounds and pass-throughs in the scoring area." The "G" stands for "total number of golds," and the "PE" is the abbreviation for the number of perfect ends.

This type of score sheet can be dittoed or mimeographed 3 or 4 to a page of 8½ X 11″ paper, and then stapled to pieces of cardboard large enough to hold one page of scoresheets across. They can be used for Double Scoring by providing each target with two scoreboards, one for each scorer. If you prefer, you can cut them into single scoresheets, so that each archer has his own for single-scoring purposes.

It is an adaptable scoresheet in that it can be used for all of the rounds listed in the rules except the F.I.T.A., York, and Hereford.

When recording, list the scores for each arrow separately, using one line of squares across the scoresheet for each end. Begin at the left, recording your highest scoring arrows and continue toward the right, recording in descending order (see Fig. 12-2). Keep in mind that if you have an even number of hits in the scoring area, your total score for them will be an even number; if you have an odd number of hits in the scoring area, the total score will be an odd number.

In the past, it was customary to put a circle around the 7's that came as a result of rebounds or pass-throughs being witnessed in the scoring area. The latest rules have eliminated this practice because it no longer serves a utilitarian purpose.

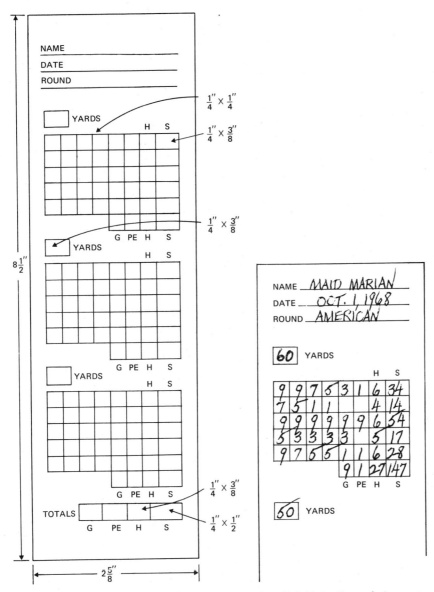

NAME _____

DATE _____

ROUND _____

☐ YARDS

$\frac{1}{4}'' \times \frac{1}{4}''$

H S

$\frac{1}{4}'' \times \frac{3}{8}''$

$\frac{1}{4}'' \times \frac{3}{8}''$

G PE H S

☐ YARDS

H S

G PE H S

☐ YARDS

H S

G PE H S

$\frac{1}{4}'' \times \frac{3}{8}''$

TOTALS

$\frac{1}{4}'' \times \frac{1}{2}''$

G PE H S

$8\frac{1}{2}''$

$2\frac{5}{8}''$

Fig. 12-1 A sample all-purpose score sheet.

NAME *MAID MARIAN*

DATE *OCT. 1, 1968*

ROUND *AMERICAN*

60 YARDS

9	9	7	5	3	1	6	34
7	5	1	1			4	14
9	9	9	9	9	9	6	54
5	3	3	3	3		5	17
9	7	5	5	1	1	6	28
					9	27	147

G PE H S

60 YARDS

Fig. 12-2 Recording archery scores.

Rules for Target Archery   139

Archery tournament equipment and accessories.

brain teasers

Whenever archers gather you'll find them talking archery in their nonshooting moments. These gab sessions often turn out to be more exciting and stimulating than shooting, and are interesting in that they give you a better understanding of archery and make you pinpoint what you know and believe. Discussion topics range from the merits of a particular bow to "what is target panic." There is an endless collection of topics to think about, form an opinion of, and investigate.

Here are a few "stumpers" that will lead to lively discussions and arguments. They could be used as lecture topics by teachers and coaches or they may be presented to a class or archer as a challenge.

1. A statement has been made: "The quality of the arrow you shoot is more important than the quality of the bow you shoot it from." Is this statement true? Why or why not?

2. Does a recurved bow have a greater cast than a long bow? Why or why not?

3. Discuss the pro's and con's of bowsight versus point-of-aim in target archery.

4. What effects will "larger than usual" feathers have on the flight of your arrows? Why?

5. What determines the size of the feathers or plastic vanes needed on your arrows?

6. Should an arrow spin in flight? Why or why not?

7. What effects, if any, will feathers with rough and frayed edges have on the flight of your arrows? Why?

8. "A crooked nock will cause greater inaccuracy in the flight of an arrow than a crooked shaft." Is this statement true or false? Why?

9. Two similar arrows are shot from the same bow. For one shot the brace-height is five inches; for the second shot it is nine inches. What effects, if any, will this difference have on the two shots? Why?

10. You release an arrow, and the string as it moves forward touches your shirt sleeve. Will this in any way affect the shot? How and why?

11. "The lower your anchor spot is, the lower your bowsight setting will be." True or false? Why?

12. List the causes of an arrow loping up and down in its flight to the target.

13. What causes an arrow to wobble from side to side in its flight to the target?

14. The weight of your bow calls for an 8-strand string and you are using a 12-strand string. What differences would it make if you changed to the 8-strand one?

15. Discuss the pro's and con's of the topic: "In target archery an anchor spot on the side of the face is better than the under-the-chin anchor."

16. "The actual number of ounces your bow string weighs has no effect upon its efficiency on your bow." True or false? Why?

17. "Tension is the greatest enemy of the target archer." True or false? Why?

18. "The archer who eliminates all torque from his bow hand will get better groups on the target face (everything else being equal) than the archer who has some torque." True or false? Why?

19. "Plastic vanes will give greater accuracy than feathers." True or false? Why?

20. "Bow strings should be waxed but never twisted." True or false? Why?

21. Discuss the pro's and con's of the three methods of bracing a bow.

archery terminology

AAC. American Archery Council

Actual draw length. The length of an arrow needed by an archer, measured at full-draw from the back of the bow to the bottom of the slit in the arrow nock.

Actual draw weight. The exact number of pounds of energy required to pull the string back to the actual draw-length of the archer.

AMO. Archery Manufacturers Organization.

Anchor point or *anchor spot.* A definite spot under the jawbone to which the index finger of the string hand must consistently be brought at the end of the draw.

Arm guard. A piece of leather or other material worn on the bow arm to protect it from string abrasion.

Arrowhead. See "Point."

Arrow plate. The area of the sight window against which the arrow rubs as it is drawn.

144

Arrow rest. A small projection placed a short distance above the grip, on which the arrow shaft rests.

Back (of the bow). The side of the bow away from the string.

Bale. Refers to the type of target made of bales of straw or excelsior. Also called "butt."

Belly (of the bow). An obsolete term. See "Face."

Bow arm. The arm that holds the bow while shooting.

Bow bracer. A device for efficiently and safely bracing a bow.

Bow hand. The hand which holds the bow while shooting.

Bowsight. An adjustable device on the bow which makes it possible for the archer to aim the point of his arrow by looking directly at the gold.

Bow stringer. See "Bow bracer."

Bow-tip protector. A piece of rubber or other material designed to protect the lower tip of the bow.

Bow weight. See "Weight."

Bowyer. A person who makes bows.

Brace. To string a bow in preparation for shooting.

Brace-height. The proper and best distance, as recommended by the manufacturer, from the pivot point to the string, which will result in the greatest efficiency of your bow. Also known as "string-height."

Broadhead. A point used in hunting, having several flat steel blades with sharpened edges.

Butt. Another name for "target." More commonly used when excelsior or straw bales make up the target.

Cant. To tip the bow right or left at full-draw.

Cast. The ability of the bow to project an arrow: the speed which a bow can impart to an arrow.

Center-shot bow. One where the arrow rests in the exact center of the upper limb rather than toward its left side.

Closed stance. A foot position on the shooting line where the line to the target runs from the toe of the right foot, through the instep of the left foot, to the target center.

Cock feather. An obsolete term. See "Index feather."

Composite bow. A bow made up of more than one substance. The back and face are often fiberglass, and the center is wood.

Creeping. Allowing the point of the arrow to move slightly forward, while aiming or at the instant of release.

Crest. The colored bands on an arrow that aid in identifying arrows on the target and elsewhere.

Crosshair sight. A type of bowsight that makes use of a circle of glass on which two fine lines cross each other at right angles.

Dead release. The act of releasing the string without having used the muscles between the shoulderblades during the draw. In this kind of release, the string fingers are forcibly pointed toward the target, and the string hand remains on its anchor spot.

Draw. The act of moving the bow string from brace-height to anchor.

End. A specified number of arrows that are to be shot before going to the target to score them. Usually six arrows which are shot in succession or in two groups of three.

Face. The side of the bow closest to the string. Formerly known as "belly."

Field Captain. The male official who is in charge of a target archery tournament.

Finger sling. A device, usually made of leather, which is attached to the index finder and the thumb of the bow hand and which extends across the back of the bow. The use of this device makes it possible for the archer to keep his bow hand fingers completely relaxed, because it keeps the bow from falling to the ground during the release and follow-through.

Finger tab. A leather device worn to protect the three string fingers from abrasion by the bow string and to give a smoother release.

F.I.T.A. Fédération Internationale de Tir à l'Arc. The organization responsible for establishing rules and standards for world championship archery meets. Also known as "Federation for International Target Archery" or "International Archery Federation."

Fletching. The feathers or plastic vanes on an arrow.

Flinching. Moving the bow arm out of the way at the instant of release in anticipation of its being hit by the string.

Foot markers. A pair of flat markers placed on the ground to mark the position of the feet on the shooting line.

Glove. See "Shooting glove."

Grip. The center section of the bow where the bow hand contacts it.

Handle. An obsolete term. See "Grip."

Handle riser. That thickened, rigid part of the bow immediately above and below the grip. Also known as "riser."

Heeling the bow. The act of pushing against the grip with a spot closer to the wrist rather than with a spot near the web of flesh between the thumb and index finger of the bow hand.

Hit. An arrow hitting within the scoring area of the target face.

Holding. Keeping the bow and arrow steady and at full-draw while completing the aiming process.

Index feather (or vane). The feather or plastic vane which is at right angles to the slit in the nock of the arrow. Formerly known as "cock feather."

Index finger. The finger with which you normally point.

Jig. A device used for holding feathers or vanes in place while fletching an arrow, or for holding the string in place while making a bow string.

Lady Paramount. The lady official in charge of a target archery tournament.

Limbs (of the bow). The working portions of the bow above and below the grip and handle-riser section.

Long bow. A bow which is comparatively straight from notch to notch along its back, having no intentionally built-in curves.

Loop. The woven or served bend in the ends of a bow string that fit into the notches when the bow is braced.

Matt (or mat). Another name for "target."

N.A.A. National Archery Association of the United States of America. This is the recognized official governing body for archery.

Nock. The device, made of plastic or other material, which provides a slit into which the string is fitted during the nocking step.

Nocking. The act of properly placing an arrow on the string in preparation for shooting.

Nocking-height. When you properly nock your arrow, the distance it is placed above square (or 90°), on the string.

Nock-locator. The stop on the string against which the arrow nock is placed when properly nocked.

Nocking point. The point on the string where the arrow is nocked. It is usually marked with a nock-locator or a pencil mark.

Notch. See "String notch."

Open stance. A foot position on the shooting line where the line to the target runs from the instep of the right foot, to the toe of the left foot, to the target center.

Overbowed. Shooting a bow which requires more strength and endurance than the archer has for continued and accurate shooting.

Overdraw. In reference to the arrow, to draw so far that the point passes the face of the bow; in reference to the bow, to draw beyond its maximum safe distance.

Overstrung bow. A bow having a string too short for it, resulting in too great a brace-height.

Peeking. The act of moving the head and/or eyes during the release and follow-through in an effort to follow the flight of the arrow.

Peep sight. A type of bowsight or string sight, having a hole through which the archer looks to the center of the gold.

Perfect end. Having all the arrows of a single end in the highest scoring circle.

Petticoat. That part of the target face outside the white scoring circle; not a part of the scoring area of the target face.

Pin sight. A type of bowsight which makes use of the head of a pin or some facsimile, such as a small dot, etc.

Pivot point. That spot on the grip which is farthest from the string when the bow is braced.

Plucking. Pulling the string hand out and away from the anchor spot as you release.

Point-of-aim. An old method of aiming the point of the arrow by using an auxiliary object that is not attached to the bow. Not in use now.

Point. That end of the arrow which enters the target first; also called "arrowhead."

Post sight. A type of bowsight which makes use of a device which projects at a right angle downward (or upward), the end of which is lined up with the aiming spot on the target face.

Pressure point. That spot on the arrow plate against which the arrow is pushed at the instant of release.

Pull. The act of removing arrows from the target.

Pushing the bow. The act of moving the bow toward the right side of the target during the act of releasing and following through.

Quiver. A receptacle for holding arrows; types used by target archers include ground, hip, back, and pocket.

Range. A distance to be shot, or an area where shooting takes place.

Recurved bow. A bow whose tips are made to bend toward the back of the bow.

Reflexed bow. A bow having straight limbs, the backs of which form an obtuse angle where they join the handle riser and grip.

Release. To let the string slip off the fingertips; to send the arrow on its way to the target.

Ring Finger: The one next to your little finger.

Riser. See "Handle-riser."

Round. Shooting a designated number of arrows at a specific size target face from one or more required distances.

Serving. A layer of thread wrapped around the bowstring to protect it from wear.

Scorers. In a tournament, the persons who are responsible for accurately recording and adding the scores for each archer at their target.

Scoring area (of the target face). That part of the target face made up of the scoring circles. Frequently colored gold, red, blue, black, and white.

Set up. The preparation of your tackle to achieve its top potential.

Shaft. The main body of the arrow.

Shooting glove. A type of hand protection which resembles a glove and which is used by some archers for string-finger protection.

Shooting line. A line designating a distance from the target.

Sight. See "Bowsight."

Sight window. That part of the upper limb just above the grip which on some bows has been cut away to allow the arrow to rest closer to the center of the bow.

Snap shooting. The act of releasing the arrow as soon as the bowsight lines up with any part of the gold on the target face, or as soon as the string touches the tip of the nose during the draw step.

Spine. The amount an arrow will bend.

Spining point. See "Pressure point."

Square stance. A foot position on the shooting line where the line to the target runs from the toes of the right foot, to the toes of the left foot, to the target center.

Stance. Maintaining proper body position while in the act of shooting.

String fingers. The three fingers which are hooked around the string in the nocking step.

String-height. See "Brace-height."

String notch. The grooves near the tip of each limb into which the loops of the bowstring fit when the bow is braced. Also called "Notch."

String pattern. The picture of the bowstring in relation to the face of the bow, as seen by the archer when he is at full-draw.

Tackle. The equipment used by an archer.

Target. The grass, straw, excelsior or other backing to which the target face is attached.

Target Captain. In a tournament, the person at each target designated to call the value of and pull the arrows for all the archers at that target.

Target face. A piece of material upon which the scoring circles are found.

Target panic. A known or unknown deficiency in shooting technique.

Throwing the bow. The act of moving the bow to the left side of the target during the act of releasing or following through.

Tip. The outermost end of the upper and lower limbs of the bow.

Timber hitch. A kind of knot used to tie the lower end of a single-looped string to the bow.

Torque. The act of putting an undesirable twist on the string or bow during the acts of drawing, anchoring, releasing and/or following through.

Toxophilite. A person fond of or devoted to archery.

Trajectory. The path of the arrow in flight.

Tune-in. The needed adjustments in your tackle to achieve perfect arrow-flight.

Underbowed. Using a bow which is too light for efficiency during its intended use.

Understrung bow. A bow having too long a string, resulting in a brace-height which is too low for efficient shooting.

Vane. A piece of thin plastic which is used in place of a feather for fletching the arrow.

Weight. The number of pounds of energy required to draw a bowstring a given distance (usually 28 inches).

Witness. In a tournament, the person at each target designated to observe the accuracy of the work being done by the Target Captain and Scorers.

Wrist sling. A device of string, leather, or other material which is attached to the bow below the grip and which is then looped over the archer's wrist. This makes it possible for him to keep his bow-hand fingers relaxed because it prevents the bow from falling to the ground during the release and follow-through.

selected references

BOOKS

Ascham, Roger, *Toxophilus*. The first book on archery! The original is dated 1545, but there are many later reprints. Much of the information is still good advice to archers. Fascinating, but slow reading.

Burke, Edmund, *The History of Archery*. New York: William Morrow and Co., 1957. A fascinating account of archery in the last 10,000 years. Amazing facts and amusing anecdotes.

Elmer, Robert P., *Target Archery*. New York: Knopf and Co., 1946. One of the most complete target archery books ever written. Accurate in all its details and packed with information that still applies.

_____, *Archery*. Philadelphia, Pa.: Penn Publishing Co., 1926. A most complete treatise on the science of target archery, its history in England and America, how to shoot, and how to make equipment.

Johnson, Frances (ed.), *Archery-Riding Guide, 1968-1970.*
Division for Girls and Womens Sports, American Association
for Health, Physical Education and Recreation, 1201 16th St.,
N.W., Washington, D.C. (A new issue is published every two
years). A book containing a series of archery-oriented articles
written by leading educators and archers. "Archery in the
Olympics"; "Ageless Archery"; "Bulletin Boards in Archery";
"Archery Conditioning Exercises"; "Success in Competition";
and others.

Keaggy, Dave, Sr., *Power Archery.* Riderwood, Md.: Archery
World Magazine, 1964 (First Edition). A dynamically written
book by one of the country's best coaches. Clearly explains
and illustrates his concept of shooting style.

_____, *Power Archery.* Drayton Plains, Mich.: Power Archery
Products, 1968 (Second Edition). New and up-to-date ideas
concerning the same basic concepts presented in the first
edition. A must for the serious archer.

Reichart, Natalie, and Gilman Keasey, *Archery.* New York:
A.S. Barnes Co., 1940. A fine presentation of the relaxed
method of shooting that is so widely used today by leading
target archers.

Roundsevelle, Phillip, *Archery Simplified.* New York: A.S.
Barnes and Co., 1931. One of the first books written for
teachers as well as archers.

Thompson, Maurice, *The Witchery of Archery.* Pinehurst,
N.C.: The Archers Company, 1928. Adventurous and exciting
tales of early archery in the United States written by one of
the men who were there. Fascinating reading for the historian,
adventurer, and archer.

PERIODICALS

Archery World. Archery Associates, Inc., Box 124, Boyer-
town, Pa., 19512. 12 issues. $5.00 per year. Official publica-
tion of the National Archery Association. Contains a variety of

articles on equipment, tournaments, club, regional, state, and national archery news. Covers all phases of archery.

Bow and Arrow. Gallant Publishing Co., 116 E. Badillo, Covina, Calif., 91722. Bimonthly. $3.00 per year. Interesting articles on all phases of archery for the beginner as well as the expert.

PAMPHLETS

American Association for Health, Physical Education and Recreation, *Archery Skills Test Manual.* Describes the test with instructions for administering it and performance percentile tables for boys and girls ages 12 to 18. Prepared by the A.A.H.P.E.R. Sport Skills Test Project. 36 pp. 75¢ American Association for Health, Physical Education and Recreation, 1201 Sixteenth St., N.W., Washington, D.C. 20036.

National Archery Association, *Junior Olympic Development Program.* An incentive program designed to create and hold the interest of the 9- to 18-year-old archer. 12 pp. 50¢ Clayton Shenk, Executive Secretary, National Archery Association, 2833 Lincoln Highway East, Ronks, Pa. 17572.

_____, *The Archer's Handbook.* Contains much information on setting up a range, conducting a tournament, organizing a club, fundamentals of shooting, rules, and rounds. 110 pp. $2.00.

_____, *Official Tournament Rules.* October, 1968, Revision. Official tournament rules for the N.A.A., Federation of International Target Archery (F.I.T.A.), N.A.A. "6 Gold" and "54" pins as well as extracts from Olympic rules. $1.25.

ARTICLES

Gervais, Lester, "Conquering the Clicker," *Archery World* *16:*44-47, January, 1967.

Hamilton, Max, "How Do Your Arrows Fly?" *Archery World* *14:*47, July, 1965.

—, "Suggestions on Shooting Vanes," *Archery World 13:*8-9, April, 1964.

—, "The Pressure Point," *Archery World 14:*31, April, 1965.

—, "Stop Bow Torque," *Archery World 15:*27, September, 1966.

Hoyt, Earl Jr., "Hoyt's Fantastic Stabilizers," *Archery World 15:*10-13, July, 1966.

—, "Torque Stabilization of the Archery Bow," *Archery World 17:*46-50, October, 1968.

Webb, Bill, "When Is Your Bow Setup Correct?" *Archery World 17:*52-56, March, 1968.

—, "Arrows Bend Around the Bow," *Archery World 15:*10-13, May, 1966.

—, "Bow Tiller Has a Pronounced Effect on Your Archery," *Archery World 15:*12-13, June, 1966.

Witt, Jack, "Controlling Your Emotions," *Archery World 17:*12, August, 1968.

—, "Do You Feel Pressure in Your Bow Arm?" *Archery World 17:*14, October, 1968.

index

index

Stance
Nock
Draw
Anchor
Aim
Release
Follow-thru